Mexico

UNITED STATES

GULF OF MEXICO

Merida
Chetumal
BR. HOND.
Campeche
GUATEMALA
Palenque
Villahermosa
Tuxtla Gutierrez
Veracruz
Jalapa
Tlaxcala
Puebla
Oaxaca
Pachuca
Mexico
Toluca
Cuernavaca
Chilpancingo
Acapulco
Queretaro
Guanajuato
Morelia
Colima
Guadalajara
Aguascalientes
San Luis Potosi
Zacatecas
Monterrey
Ciudad Victoria
Saltillo
Torreón
Durango
SIERRA MADRE ORIENTAL
SIERRA MADRE OCCIDENTAL
MEXICO
Culiacan
Mazatlán
(Rio Grande)
Ciudad Juárez
Rio Bravo
Chihuahua
Rio Conchos
Rio Yaqui
Nogales
Hermosillo
La Paz
GULF OF CALIFORNIA
Mexicali
Tijuana
Ensenada

PACIFIC OCEAN

N.

0   100   200   300   400   500 Miles

A CONCISE HISTORY OF

Mexico

by Victor Alba

CASSELL · LONDON

CASSELL & COMPANY LTD
35 Red Lion Square, London WC1R 4SG
Sydney, Auckland, Toronto, Johannesburg

First published in Great Britain 1973
(I.S.B.N. 0 304 29238 9)
Manufactured in the United States of America

CHAPTER I

A WORLD
IN ITSELF

When Christopher Columbus made his first landfall in the new world that was to be the Americas, he believed, as we all know, that he had reached India and had no idea that he had discovered a new continent. Thirty years later, when Hernán Cortés disembarked on the coast of Mexico, he knew he had discovered a country but did not realize that he had also discovered a separate world within a world. For Mexico, in 1519, was a world in itself, cut off from the rest of the globe and even from the rest of the Western Hemisphere. It had its own history, peoples, and languages, and the inhabitants knew of nothing beyond this world and believed they were alone in the universe. And, in a manner of speaking, Mexico has continued to be a world rather than simply a country.

Mexico lies roughly on the same latitude as the Sahara Desert, but it is altitude rather than closeness to the equator that is the decisive influence on the climate—and ultimately the human geography of the country. Chains of steep mountains parallel the two coasts—the Pacific is buttressed by the Sierra Madre Occidental and the Gulf of Mexico by the Sierra Madre Oriental (part of a system which northward

In a detail from his mural depicting the Pre-Columbian civilization of Veracruz, Diego Rivera shows a merchant greeting a Totonac chief.

becomes the Rocky Mountains and extends to Alaska). Between these chains hangs a vast central plateau. In the north where the mesa averages six thousand feet above sea level it is today a semiarid desert; farther south it rises still higher to eight thousand feet, the climate becoming cooler and more moist as it approaches a vast volcanic zone. The Valley of Mexico, an oval basin extending some fifty miles in the center of this region, is the richest and most densely populated part of the country and the scene of many of the decisive occurrences of the history we are relating. Montezuma's Aztec capital—ultimately Mexico City—would be built here on one of the four large shallow lakes that once dominated the landscape. Nearby an east-west belt of volcanoes crosses the country—including Popocatepetl, Iztaccihuatl, and Citlaltepetl, which at 18,700 feet is the most majestic of them all. Mountain and valley country continues in the south, sloping down to the Isthmus of Tehuantepec and the thickly forested peninsula of Yucatán.

All in all Mexico presents a very rugged profile, one that would seem inconducive to the growth of a great civilization. Even the narrow coastal margins of flat lands that skirt each mountain range are poor in this respect, with a hot, steamy climate that is more hospitable to disease-carrying mosquitoes than to human inhabitants. Called the *tierra caliente* (the hot land), it supports only tropical crops and then with considerable effort, since there is a constant struggle against the jungle's encroachment. In other areas, where the terrain is suitable for agriculture, the rainfall is scant and the rivers unreliable. Consequently, only 7 per cent of Mexican land is arable.

The early European explorers, accustomed to the intimate dimensions of Europe, were astonished at the immensity of this strange new environment, a land in which one was forever climbing or descending. They were equally baffled by the customs, language, and society of the people they encountered. A surprise awaited the visitors beyond every mountain pass, for in a land in which travel was so difficult, the peoples had developed local patterns of living largely in isolation from one another, and the apparent differences among them were great.

Fortunately for future historians, some of Cortés' soldiers had been educated and took an interest in writing down what they saw, although they were at times annihilating examples of indigenous culture faster than they could take note of them through wanton destruction of temples, the burning of religious objects, the melting down of precious metals, and many bloody battles. Cortés' company also included men of the Church and there were numbers of friars who came in the years immediately following the first invasion, and they made it their purpose to learn the local languages so that they could convert the natives. Little by little observers amassed a considerable body of legends, songs, historical accounts, and other documents. In time this information contributed to the first serious historical works about Mexico; centuries later archaeologists excavating and interpreting ruins, pottery, sculpture, hieroglyphics, and the like were able to fill in these first facts in greater detail. The history which emerges may be compared in its main lines to that of the classical world of the Mediterranean.

As in that better-known history, we must begin by solving the problem of the origins of Mexico's earliest inhabitants. There have been many theories and, though specialists are now generally agreed that the first settlers came from Asia, there are still those—the man in the street in particular—who prefer other explanations. Perhaps the favorite theory, introduced by some early Spanish missionaries and maintained by some later nineteenth-century scholars, is that the indigenous Mexicans were members of one of the lost tribes of Israel or emigrants from the Egypt of the pharaohs.

If there is now general agreement that the Americas' Indians came from Asia, there is less agreement on when the migrations took place. By means of radiocarbon dating of organic materials found in association with spear tips, chipped stone implements, and other human artifacts, archaeologists can with certainty place man in Mexico as early as 10,000 B.C., but there is less secure evidence that could push his date of arrival back as far as 30,000 B.C. Either way, it is conjectured that the crossing was made over the Bering Strait, really a land bridge in ancient times, during some phase of the glacial period when the ice sheets that covered vast areas of the Americas had receded.

These paleolithic travelers were hunters of big game—and they must have followed the herds southward and eastward until their settlements were scattered over the length and breadth of the continent. In Mexico the big game phase gave way to small game and wild food

OVERLEAF: *Monte Albán in Oaxaca was a ceremonial center from 500 B.C. to A.D. 900. Zapotecs and their successors worshiped in the pyramids shown here.*

gathering as the northern glaciers retreated and the climate changed accordingly, around 7000 B.C. Man, who had arrived in this hemisphere with such primitive skills as fire-making, flint-chipping, and hunting, as well as some shared ideas about the supernatural and kin group organization, now began to show signs of greater sophistication.

The harsh terrain of Mexico assured that many different tribal cultures would develop independently in several parts of Mexico, though their various stages of maturation would be duplicated everywhere in broad outline. Tehuacán in the modern state of Puebla serves as a convenient example of early man's social evolution. By 6000 B.C. the men of this 6,000-foot-high valley were raising a primitive strain of corn—thereafter the staple of the Mexican diet—as well as chili peppers, gourds, beans, and other plants. A little more than five thousand years ago they were sufficiently in control of their food supply to settle seasonally in villages, increase their population markedly, and begin to develop a culture with a distinctive system of religious observance, pottery-making, and the like. Even with their primitive methods of cultivation, these first farmers could harvest enough corn for a whole year by working only 180 days.

With the establishment of the village and a more dependable food supply came the possibilities of still wider social organization and the crystallization of cultural traditions. That phase, now designated the Pre-Classic, stretched from 2000 B.C. to A.D. 300. Ceremonial centers shared by many villages began to appear. They were not cities but rather dwelling places of religious leaders, who were the first tribal chiefs. Thus political power and spiritual power were one, with ritual the organizing force in Tehuacán and elsewhere. In architecture, in pottery, in the development of a calendar and a system of notation, even in the playing of a game involving a rubber ball and two opposing teams, religion was to be the prime motivation.

It was long fashionable to think of Mexico's Indian civilization as being a relatively late phenomenon in human history. The Aztecs for example, trace their existence as a tribal entity back to a time concurrent with the European Renaissance; the ancient Mayas to a time roughly parallel to the fall of the Roman Empire. It was assumed for lack of previous information that all else was a modest and predictable prologue to these flowerings. But in recent years the archaeological

clock—and the history of Mexico with it—has had to be dramatically
revised as the story of the Olmecs is unraveled. These Pre-Classic
people once lived in the wet, swampy, tropical lowlands of what are
today the Gulf Coast states of Veracruz and Tabasco. We now know
that they were Mexico's first and indeed the Western Hemisphere's
first people to attain a civilization and that they accomplished this at
least a thousand years before Christ. Also, they are widely regarded as
the common ancestors of all those civilizations and empires that followed, their culture the heritage of later times and peoples.

The Olmecs are known to us principally through remains at three
sites: La Venta, Tres Zapotes, and San Lorenzo. Undoubtedly the most
arresting discoveries have been a number of colossal heads, carved of
huge basalt boulders weighing up to eighteen tons by sculptors who
had no metal tools. The basalt, which is not native to the sites where
the heads were found, is thought to have been dragged through the
mangrove swamps from Tuxtla Mountain some sixty to eighty miles
away. The portraits are probably of Olmec kings and the curious hel-
mets perhaps a sort of headgear worn in a ritual ball game. Owing to
the lush jungle in which they lay discarded for twenty centuries and
more, they were easily overlooked by early archaeologists as were the
Olmecs' pyramidal earthworks; burial mounds perhaps, these highly
ambitious constructions are just now being revealed as the forest lands
are cut back.

Features of the Olmec culture including a fertility god who took the
form of a jaguar, conventions in sculptural style, language, and perhaps the prototype of the calendar were passed on to later Mexican
civilizations by traders and warriors. The Olmecs have a place in history rather like that of the Minoans who foreshadowed the ancient
Greeks; in this equation the Olmecs' Greeks would be the Mayas. Near
the end of the Pre-Classic period as the Olmec civilization began to
decline, two other great centers were rising inland: Teotihuacán in the
Valley of Mexico (near modern-day Mexico City) and Monte Albán
at Oaxaca. Both were true urban centers, not simply ceremonial sites,
with genuine political and mercantile functions. Teotihuacán rose
circa 300 B.C. in the region of huge shallow lakes. The Teotihuacanos,
whose tribal identity has never been established, learned the skills of
irrigation, and the city prospered so as an agricultural center that by

The map at the top of the page shows important Middle American archaeological sites. Labels visible on the map include: GULF OF MEXICO, TOLTEC, TAJIN, CHICHEN ITZA, TOTONAC, MAYAPAN, UXMAL, TULUM, KABAH, SAYIL, TULA, LABNA, TEOTIHUACAN, ATILCO, TENOCHTITLAN, LAKE TEXCOCO, ZTEC, VALLEY OF MEXICO, CHOLULA, TRES ZAPOTES, MAYA, MIXTEC, LA VENTA, OLMEC, PALENQUE, UAXACTUN, BRITISH HONDURAS, PIEDRAS NEGRAS, LAKE PETEN, TIKAL, MONTE ALBAN, MITLA, MEXICO, BONAMPAK, ZAPOTEC, N, SCALE, 0 25 50 75 MILES, PACIFIC OCEAN, GUATEMALA, COPAN, HONDURAS, KAMINALJUYU, EL SALVADOR

A.D. 300 an estimated 100,000 people lived within its eight-square-mile precincts. And, as a city, it generated a class structure—priests, warriors, merchants, artisans, farmers, and the like. Regarded as the most powerful political and cultural force in all Middle America during the early Classic stage, Teotihuacán's influence seems to have been felt as far away as the country of the Mayas. It was surmised by the Aztecs, who came centuries later, that the city was the creation of the gods, and indeed the two tremendous masonry pyramids dedicated to the Sun God and the Moon Goddess and a temple honoring the god who brought civilization, the feathered serpent Quetzalcoatl, would give many pause. Teotihuacán fell to an unknown enemy around A.D. 650 and political power in the region shifted.

The city of Monte Albán was the creation of the Zapotecs, though it is very much Olmec-derived. Sculptural relief which decorates the base of one of their most ancient structures (c. 500 B.C.) depicts human figures which are probably captives prepared for sacrificial rites. Monte Albán continued to dominate the valleys of the Oaxaca region for many centuries, existing throughout the Classic period as a ceremonial center even after Mixtec Indians had replaced Zapotecs as its rulers.

The map above shows important Middle American archaeological sites dating from 1500 B.C. to A.D. 1300.

As time went on Olmec influence in the Oaxaca valley waned but it reappears in another more distant corner of Mexico, in Yucatán, among the Mayas, whose civilization reached its full flowering slightly before A.D. 300 and ended around 900. The origin of the Mayas remains uncertain, with evidence of Mayan settlement dating back as far as 1400 B.C. or even earlier, but the affinity of the Mayan language family with that of the Olmec suggests that the first Mayas may have migrated northeastward from Olmec territory. In any case the many artistic similarities which are apparent would seem to confirm some ancestral relationship. But the brilliance and extent of Mayan civilization gives it a character all its own. The Mayas are justly celebrated as mathematicians and astronomers for they not only knew the exact length of the year, using a calendar that predated the West's Gregorian calendar by 1,300 years, but they also calculated the course of the moon and the sun and their eclipses. They had conceived an advanced system of numbers based on 20 (counting toes as well as fingers), using positional numbers and zero—an abstraction that European man did not discover until the end of the Middle Ages and then only by borrowing it from the Hindu astronomers. This number system also made possible the Mayas' dating of their own history. Perhaps even more significant, they developed glyphs with which they were able to write much more than kings' names and dates. Diego de Landa, the sixteenth-century bishop of Yucatán, observed, "these people also made use of certain characters or letters, with which they wrote in their books, their ancient affairs and their sciences, and with these . . . they understood their affairs and made others understand them and taught them." Sadly, Landa's respect for their accomplishment was outweighed by his suspicion of the contents. "We found a great number of books in these characters, and, as they contained nothing in which there was not to be seen superstition and the lies of the devil, we burned them all, which they regretted to an amazing degree and caused them affliction." (The books which he referred to were codices written on bark paper, the same material used for some clothing.) Glyphs were also inscribed on steles, temple walls, and on small objects including pottery, jade, bone, and shell. The search for the key to these writings continues—so far about one quarter of the hieroglyphics have been translated, but as new computerized techniques of linguistic analysis are applied, it seems entirely possible that the still-mysterious Mayas will become a great deal more familiar to us.

During the six-hundred-year era of Mayan splendor the achievements of its civilization spread widely throughout Yucatán, Guatemala, and Honduras, a territory as large as that of modern Italy. City-states comparable to those of the early Greeks, rather than a centralized empire, held the region together in a loose, remarkably peaceful association. Tikal, Palenque, Chichén Itzá, Copán, Bonampák, and Uxmal remain among the most spectacular sites. Based on archaeological discoveries there were at least 116 such centers. As the jungle agriculture which sustained the Mayas was of the primitive slash-and-burn variety rather than the intensive cultivation practiced on the more rewarding soil of Tenochtitlán (the ancient name of Mexico City), these communities were much less highly organized than those of the Zapotecs. Hence the idea of "cities" is here something of a misnomer. Each center, usually built on a height, contained a pyramid surmounted by a temple, monumental stairways, an astronomical observatory, ceremonial courtyards, altars, and the like. The farmer population, which means most of the people, lived in small hamlets at some remove from the acropolis. Their dwellings were usually fashioned of wood and thatch, very like those still to be seen in the region.

As the agricultural pattern suggests, Mayan technology did not keep pace with Mayan artistry. Metallurgy and metal tools were still unknown—no important metal deposits existed there. Nor had they developed the wheel as an aid to transport. Draft animals and any other sort of domesticated animals except the dog were also unknown.

Sometime around A.D. 900, lowland Mayan civilization suffered a rapid decline; evidence lies in the fact that no new ceremonial centers were built, no steles relating the passage of kings carved, no new codices written in the southern portion of the Mayan lowlands where the finest work had traditionally been produced. The cause is still unknown although there is good reason to suspect that the population growth suddenly exceeded the people's ability to feed themselves. The soil was so poor that every two years a plot had to be abandoned for another and the arduous task of burning and cutting away more of the rain forest repeated. Perhaps the specter of famine and popular uprisings forced them to disperse; or attacks by other peoples who

took advantage of their weakness. Only in the Guatemala highlands did the culture continue to flourish, though it was now subject to repeated conflict as centers became increasingly competitive among one another. By the time the Spaniards came, petty warfare had all but destroyed the highland Mayan civilization as well.

With the burning of Teotihuacán and the abandonment of Monte Albán and the lowland Mayan sites, the Classic period of ancient Mexico verged into the Post-Classic. The generally accepted date for the changeover is A.D. 900. Meanwhile, other multiethnic tribes were preparing to move into these civilized regions from the arid north. Barbarians by comparison, they were still hunters and gatherers, and many of them spoke a language that would be ancestral to the Aztecs' Nahuatl. Of these the Toltecs became the dominant tribe, founding their great city of Tula (in Hidalgo state) sometime in the tenth cen-

A multicolored stone carving of Quetzalcoatl, the Feathered Serpent, adorns a temple in his honor at Teotihuacán, northeast of Mexico City.

tury. For almost two hundred years they remained unchallenged from without, but early on an internal struggle for control of government shook its foundations. This schism occurred when separate military and religious factions arose and contended for Toltec leadership. Aztec legend, an apparent confirmation, tells of a struggle between the benign god Quetzalcoatl and the magician Tezcatlipoca, Lord of the Night. The god of darkness was victorious and Quetzalcoatl went into exile toward the "divine sea," whence he sailed eastward. In reality Mayan chronicles indicate that around the year 987 a Toltec ruler named Topiltzin Quetzalcoatl was forced to leave Tula. With his followers he crossed the Bay of Campeche and landed in Yucatán, taking many abandoned Mayan cities including Chichén Itzá, which was rebuilt about this time. For two centuries the Yucatán enjoyed peace and prosperity under the government of a league of cities known to historians as the New Mayan Empire. Meanwhile, the Toltecs of Tula, having cast their lot with the forces of war, became the leading military force in central Mexico. They proved to be great assimilators and their brief reign vigorous and innovative. They were the first Mexicans to be metalworkers, using skills apparently transmitted from Peru and Ecuador. But the split which had divided Tula and attacks by still another wave of northern barbarians—the Chichimecs, or Dog People—brought down the Toltec dynasty around A.D. 1200.

The Chichimecs, who also spoke Nahuatl, had a ruder culture but they knew how to use the bow and arrow, which gave them a tremendous advantage over the settled peoples who fought with stone axes and spears. Adopting the life style and culture of those they overcame, the various Chichimec tribes founded city-states in the region of Lake Texcoco and struggled among themselves for hegemony. Among the contenders were the Mexicas—or Aztecs, as they were later called. Of their origins Aztec legend says that they were the last people to invade central Mexico. Their homeland in the north they called Aztlán, and they told of following their tribal god of war Huitzilopochtli into the Valley of Mexico, where they appropriated land in and around the western edge of the marshy lake. There on an island they founded Tenochtitlán, whose name signified Place of the Cactus in the Rock, for it had been foretold that they should settle where they found an eagle with a snake in its beak perched on a nopal. (This image of the cactus, the eagle, and the serpent is preserved today in the Mexican national insignia.) The year, according to the Aztec calendar, was 1325. At first the Aztecs were vassals to other, older city-states, but, by selling their services wisely, they built their way toward greater and greater strength. The Tepanec princes of Azcapotzalco accepted the Aztecs as allies. In 1428, after the Tepanecs had subdued the rest of their neighbors, the Aztecs turned on them, and through conquest gained control of the Valley of Mexico. Thus was born the Aztec Empire, culturally bound to age-old traditions of central Mexico, but politically much ahead of its predecessors.

As tribute poured into the emperor's treasury, the city of Tenochtitlán grew in size and magnificence. Vast public works, chiefly devoted to raising artificial islands in Lake Texcoco, building causeways, and reclaiming swamps, were undertaken. Aztec traders swarmed over the country, league officials following them to collect taxes, often in the currency of cacao pods, plumes, and textiles, and the princes of weaker states from the Gulf Coast to the Pacific yielded. The Aztecs rarely sought political dominion over the outlying states—tribute and recognition were enough and any state so foolish as to deny them was usually looted and brought to submission. (Cortés would exploit the resentment of these unwilling satellites to bring down the Aztec emperor Montezuma II.)

Religious life permeated Aztec society and Aztec priests were its rulers. Ceremonials were treated with great importance. Seemingly more possessed of their faith than their forebears, the Aztecs celebrated every feast day in their calendar with gestures more elaborate than ever before. Human sacrifice, while not original with the Aztecs, was carried out on a grander scale. To make sure that the sun would rise, that the earth would be fertile, that the rains would come when needed, and victory be forever their reward, quantities of victims were needed to propitiate the appropriate gods (the Aztecs recognized more than sixty in their pantheon). Ritual cannibalism appears to have been a feature of the celebrations. Selection as a candidate for sacrifice carried considerable prestige, for such a person was destined to be made one with divinity. But most victims were gathered from tributaries and enemies. One means was the "Flower War," a ritual battle staged between neighboring cities for the sole purpose of recruit-

Pre-Columbian pottery artifacts: (top to bottom) Mayan demon, seated Aztec woman, painted lid; (right) Mayan ritual figure

ing sacrificial victims. Killing was forbidden and the mock battle went on until the prearranged number of captives had been collected.

Intellectual life, as heir to so many cultures, flourished among the Aztecs. Its survivals include poems and "words of the ancients," or proverbs, and it appears that the priests carried on very complex theological and ethical discussions. (The Texcoco monarch Nezahualcoyotl was more highly regarded as a maker of poems and songs than as a ruler.)

Prosperity increased. Under Montezuma I an aqueduct carrying sweet water from the springs of Chapultepec to the central city was built. A massive dike held back the lakes in the rainy season. From the south came skill in working copper, iron, and silver, though these metals were used only for making luxury objects and not for tools. The ruling groups—priests, warriors, and traders we would call exporters—indulged in luxuries of clothing and of plumes, sumptuous palaces, gardens with waterfalls and pools. It is possible that the Aztec chieftains lived a more elegant life than that of European potentates of the same era, although they had less practical knowledge. Tenochtitlán was not only larger than most European cities, but enjoyed greater order, better sanitation, and more public services than the cities of the Old World, most of which still had no sewage system and no municipal police.

The state was imperialistic, dominating the surrounding settlements and compelling them to federate with it and to pay tribute. Only one people successfully resisted the Aztecs, the Tarascos of Michoacán, in the northeast. Their capital, Tzintzuntzan, on the shores of Lake Pátzcuaro, received embassies and tribute from other peoples trying to evade Aztec dominion—among them the Mixtecs of Oaxaca, who had driven out the Zapotecs of Monte Albán in the fourteenth century.

The Aztecs' social organization was by far the most advanced known in pre-colonial Mexico, though elements of it could be found in all others. Within the inner circle of the Aztec empire, a rigid class structure was maintained. Some twenty calpulli, or clans, controlled the city of Tenochtitlán, each one supervising the government, schools, or "houses of youth," temples, and markets of its own autonomous district. Each clan, consisting of a number of fami-

A page from an Aztec codex catalogs pictorially some of the tribute, such as costumes and fabrics, collected from a subject tribe every eighty days.

lies, was directed by a trio of leaders whose responsibilities—roughly speaking, executive, military, and judicial—extended to state functions. The city as a whole was divided into four quarters, a number of clans in each, and a man from each quarter chosen to represent his district on a four-man council of state. In theory they even chose the emperor, or Chief of Men as he was known, though by custom one clan was thought to be the bearer of almost all the semidivine rulers. The Aztecs practiced monogamy, and women were theoretically equal to men, though in practice they were subjugated. All youths might be called into military service by the nobles or warriors. The land belonged to the clan but the families of warriors or priests had more of it, and also had serfs and slaves to cultivate it.

The ancient Mexicans as nomads had enjoyed equality among themselves, but once settled, differences of wealth had arisen, because of the size and quality of the lands they received or through the booty which they were able to keep and hand on to their heirs. War determined, also, some specialization of labor and the rise of professions —armorers, makers of plumed objects, et cetera—and this, in turn, led to the formation of guilds not very unlike the medieval European ones, some of them for women. Each guild was assigned to its own quarters in Tenochtitlán. Artisans were free, owing only military tribute to the city. The *tlacotli,* the man expelled from his clan as a judicial punishment or for violating some tradition, was also technically free, although his piece of land was forfeit, and he was obliged to work for someone else to support himself. He was not a slave, for he had the right to change patrons, and his children continued to belong to the clan. Legally, this man was not a part of society, which ignored him; he was a nonperson.

Besides the tlacotli there was the slave captured in war. Often the number of prisoners of war exceeded the quota of men needed for religious sacrifices, in which case they were put to work in the priests' and warriors' fields, in their houses, or in public works. The least fortunate had the task of transporting merchandise on their backs, since the Aztecs (as has been mentioned) did not know the use of the wheel for transportation (although they used it for other purposes) and had no beasts of burden.

This technological blind spot should not be construed as an indica-

A native artist depicts the coronation of Emperor Montezuma II, shown here receiving the crown of his office from a high priest.

tion that the Aztecs were a primitive people. They had developed—in the area of religion, for example—a sophisticated outlook on life. An Aztec who survived the conquest, Hernando Alvarado Tezozómoc, wrote in his native Nahuatl a *Crónica Mexicayotl* (Mexican Chronicle) which was later translated into Spanish. In it he tells how one of the lords of the Valley of Mexico, Huitzilihuitl, fell in love with the daughter of the lord of Cuernavaca. "His heart was in Cuernavaca, there alone, and he immediately sent word to her parents asking for her hand."

But the lord of Cuernavaca was a witch doctor. "He called on all the spiders as well as the centipede, the serpent, the bat and the scorpion, ordering all of them to guard his very famous virgin daughter so that no one might enter there and no villain dishonor her. She was locked in and well guarded, with every species of wild beast at all the palace doors. Because of this there was great fear and no one approached the palace. The kings of all the towns solicited this princess, because they wished to marry her with their sons. But the father accepted none of the proposals." When the envoys sent by the lord of Mexico related their message, the lord of Cuernavaca asked, "What does he say? What can he give her? . . . that which the water yields, that is, will he dress her as he is attired in clothing made from linen of the waters? And what foods will he give her? Or is his home possibly like this where there is everything, meats, and delicious fruits, the indispensable cotton and elegant garments? Go tell all this to your king before you return here." Upon hearing of the lord of Cuernavaca's response, Huitzilihuitl became very discouraged. But the god Tezcatlipoca came to him in his dreams and said, "Do not grieve, for I have come to tell you what you must do in order to win the virgin. Make a spear and a small net and with them you will go to the house of the lord of Cuernavaca where his daughter is kept under guard. Make also a beautiful staff. Decorate it carefully, paint it well, inserting in the center a precious stone, shining handsomely. You must go there along the borders where you will cast the cane in the center of which is the precious stone, and it will fall to earth where the daughter of the king of Cuernavaca is being protected and then we shall have her." Huitzilihuitl obeyed the god's orders, and when the virgin saw the cane she pulled it from the ground, broke it in two, and saw inside the shining gem. Curious to know if the stone was good, she bit it. But she swallowed it by mistake and, unable to get the stone out, she found herself pregnant. All this went just as the god had planned, and since Huitzilihuitl was responsible for her pregnancy, the lord of Cuernavaca offered him his daughter's hand.

This, although it may appear to be a love story, is much more: it is a political lesson. The maiden, says Ignacio Bernal, who quotes this legend, was greedy, for she wanted to know if the stone was valuable, and so was the lord of Mexico, for what he really wanted was the abundant cotton harvest of Cuernavaca.

Obviously, this was a complex society, with nothing of the simple or primitive about its culture. The Aztecs called themselves "the people of the sun," and converted the ancient central Mexican legend of Quetzalcoatl's defeat and withdrawal by sea into a doctrine of salvation, according to which Quetzalcoatl, now conceived as white-skinned, would return from the east to rule his people once more. This played right into the hands of the Spaniards, since they were white and came from the east, but it would not have been enough to assure their victory. There were many other factors in their favor.

One was the discontent among the peoples subject to (or resistant to) the Aztecs. Another was the dissatisfaction at the very heart of the Aztec society. As this society had become more and more complex, new tensions had arisen. The traders, particularly those who maintained relations with the peoples of the distant south, were displeased at the priests' and warriors' monopoly of power and wanted not only a part of the wealth but also a share of the right to govern. These aspirations of what now would be called a new class had provoked a hidden social crisis among the Aztecs, and this crisis weakened their capacity to resist.

Although the Aztecs were physically different from Europeans, being darker, and were clad with more luxury, if less clothing, and although their language and religion were different, their experience was not fundamentally unlike that the Romans had faced in the decadence of their empire. For the Aztecs, the Spaniards played the part the Germans had played vis-à-vis Rome—they were the barbarians.

CHAPTER II

A VERY
NEW SPAIN

T wo quite ordinary Spaniards, a soldier named Gonzalo Guerrero and the priest Jerónimo de Aguilar, were among a small boatload of survivors who in 1512 landed on the east coast of Yucatán after their ship had been wrecked in the Gulf of Mexico. Most of the party died from their ordeal, but these two caught the fancy of their captors and were made slaves. The pair won freedom, Guerrero even marrying a Mayan woman, and they became so closely identified with the Indians' life, culture, and language that when the Spanish captain Francisco de Córdoba discovered Yucatán in 1517, Guerrero helped the Indians defend themselves against the captain and his party.

Hernán Cortés, who led the initial expedition that conquered Mexico, was, like many conquistadors, a younger son of a poor *hidalgo* family. He had spent two years at the noted University of Salamanca, but before completing his studies succumbed to the temptations of the American adventure, and made his way to Cuba. There, being intelligent, impetuous, and shrewd, he soon won fairly important appointments, and became secretary to the governor of the island. From this vantage, he persuaded the governor to let him organize an expedition,

Cortés, armored and astride a white horse, clashes with Aztec warriors in a mural by Diego Rivera located in the Palace of Cortés, Cuernavaca.

and rounded up more than five hundred men, sixteen of them mounted, and fourteen cannon. That made the governor uneasy, for this was a formidable force in such a place, and he withdrew his permission. Cortés pretended not to understand, and embarked in February, 1519. He was then thirty-four years old.

Landing in Yucatán, he struck up with the shipwrecked priest Aguilar, who became his interpreter and counselor in relations with the natives. Shortly afterward, Cortés received, as a token of friendship, the daughter of an Indian *cacique,* Malintzin, or Doña Marina as the Spaniards called her. (Present-day Mexicans know her as Malinche, from which evolved the word *malinchista* to designate those who show a preference for things foreign.) Malinche learned Spanish, taught Cortés the local language, and bore him several sons. Cortés for his part had first of all seen to it that she was baptized.

There were two factions in the little troop, one loyal to Cortés and the other to the governor of Cuba. To rid himself of these divided loyalties, and to guarantee that the riches he expected to gather would not go to benefit the governor, the conquistador decided to establish a town—Veracruz. According to Spanish law, as citizens of a town, the Cortés party assumed certain rights of self-government, and were responsible to the Crown. The royal authority then became vested in the *cabildo,* or local assembly of the inhabitants, and not in the governor. However, Cortés, fearing that the governor's partisans might compel him to return to Cuba, beached his fleet. Legend has it that he burned his ships, but in reality he merely ran them aground in such a way that in case of danger he would be able to float them again. Cortés was daring, but discreet.

In mid-August, 1519, Cortés and his entourage left the coast for the long overland march to the Aztec capital and the long-awaited meeting with Montezuma II. After two weeks, the Spanish column crossed into Tlaxcala, one of three kingdoms which still steadfastly retained a measure of independence from the Aztecs. Cortés attempted to convince the Tlascalans that he wished only to pass in peace through their land, but the proud Tlascalans engaged the Spaniards in several bloody battles before they allowed them to enter the capital. Cortés, whose skill as a diplomat was growing with each day, granted the Indians amnesty in return for their promise of support against their traditional enemies. Cortés was at the same time sending reassurances of friendship to Montezuma and, still uninvited, he resumed his march.

Montezuma had been kept informed by his scouts and he sent emissaries to Cortés, bearing gifts and promises of tribute but requesting that he go away. Cortés plodded on. He reached the holy city of Cholula, in which, it was said, there were 365 temples, one for every day of the year. To magnify the terror already caused by his firearms and horses, neither of which these inland Indians had ever seen, he cold-bloodedly massacred some six thousand citizens. Then, with the aid of the Tlascalans, he continued his march. Suspicious of ambush, he avoided the well-traveled routes to the capital, following tortuous trails through the mountains. On November 8, three months after they had struck inland, they came to a place since named Paso de Cortés, between two volcanoes in whose shadow lay Tenochtitlán, on Lake Texcoco.

The Spaniards, mostly rude soldiers except for a few educated men and priests, had gone from surprise to surprise during those ninety days of travel through the jungle. They saw strange animals and plants unknown in Europe. They learned to bear high temperatures while clad in their armor, and their velvet or homespun clothing. They suffered from cold that was more intense than any they had felt in Spain. They had become used to the appearance of the Indians, who had first seemed strange, with their small stature and aquiline noses, their glossy hair and beardless faces, and their bronze skins. In idle moments the captains even adopted the comfortable native tunic and white cape that protected them from the heat and the mosquitoes. They learned to enjoy the strange, perfumed and sweetish tropical fruits. When they had nothing to do, they played a game similar to basketball in which they tossed a rubber ball through a stone hoop.

But nothing had prepared them for this view of Tenochtitlán, which seemed to float on the lake, like so many different islets, and the satellite cities around its shores. Confronting the thousands of pagan warriors with gold necklaces and bracelets were scarcely five hundred of the astounded Spaniards, with a few cannon, their harquebuses, and a dozen horses. Only a blend of ambition, adventurousness, and a conviction of superiority can explain their daring to go down the mountains and enter the city, larger than any they had ever imagined.

Cortés' redheaded captain Pedro de Alvarado is shown wearing the red armband of the Spanish Order of Santiago in a posthumous portrait.

Bernal Díaz del Castillo was one of the captains of the little Spanish force. Years later, when he was retired and old, he wrote a chronicle of the expedition in which he reported his impressions of Tenochtitlán:

"We were amazed and said that it was like the enchantments they tell of in the legend of Amadis. . . . And some of our soldiers even asked whether the things we saw were not a dream. . . .

"And then when we entered . . . Iztapalapa, the appearance of the palaces in which they lodged us! How spacious and well built they were, of beautiful stone work and cedar wood, and the wood of other sweet scented trees, with great rooms and courts, wonderful to behold, covered with awnings of cotton cloth. . . .

"We went to the orchard and garden, which was a wonderful thing to see and walk in, that I was never tired of looking at the diversity of the trees, and noting the scent which each one had, and the paths full of roses and flowers, and the many fruit trees . . . and the pond of fresh water. . . . Great canoes were able to pass into the garden from the lake. . . .And all was cemented and very splendid with many kinds of stone [monuments] with pictures on them, which gave much to think about. Then the birds of many kinds . . . which came into the pond. I say again that I stood looking at it and thought that never in the world would there be discovered other lands such as these. . . . Of all these wonders that I then beheld, today all is overthrown and lost, nothing left standing."

One of the founders of Mexican historiography, the eighteenth-century Jesuit Francisco Javier Clavijero, gave this description of the houses in Tenochtitlán:

"The houses of the rich were of stone and lime with several tall chambers and great patios. The flat roofs were made of good wood, the walls were so well polished that the first Spaniards to see them thought they were made of silver. The floors were of mortar, perfectly leveled and polished. Many houses had towers and roof crests, an atrium with trees, and an orchard with pools. The largest houses had two openings, one leading to the street, the other to the canal or canoe passage. Neither entrance had wooden doors because doors were not used, believing that their houses were well defended by the severity of their laws against thieves. To keep people from peering inside they had the entrance covered with a reed curtain."

And Cortés himself, in a letter to the king, speaks of his wonder at the sight of the Aztec markets:

"This city had many plazas, where there are perpetual markets and business of buying and selling. There is a plaza which is twice as large as that of the city of Salamanca, all surrounded with arcades, where every day more than 60,000 people come to buy and sell; where all the kinds of merchandise that there is in this land can be found. There are foods, jewels of gold and silver, of lead, tin, copper, stone, things as you can find in this land, all which for prolixity and failure of memory, and because I do not know many of the names of the products, I do not mention them here. Every kind of merchandise is sold in its own place and in this they have much order. They sell everything by count and by measures, and up to now I have not seen anything sold by weight."

Montezuma II had no wish to fight these strange beings. He believed, like many of his subjects, that Cortés was Quetzalcoatl. He thought also that gifts could persuade the Spaniards to withdraw. After a week's stay, Cortés received news that the Indians of the coast had attacked Veracruz. He took the emperor as a hostage.

But he derived no benefit from this move, for he learned that the governor of Cuba was sending some eight hundred men against him. Leaving a small garrison in the Aztec capital, he set off for the coast to encounter the governor's soldiers, and sent out secret agents to tell the governor's men about Montezuma's wealth. As a result, when the moment of battle arrived, there was hardly any struggle, for Cortés' forces were enlarged by the mass desertion of the expeditionaries who had been sent to capture him.

But upon his return to the capital, in June, 1520, he found the Spaniards besieged by Indians who were angry because they had interrupted a religious ceremony and had insulted the Aztec priests. Cortés tried to appease the Indians by having Montezuma address them from the balcony behind which the Spaniards had taken refuge. A stone thrown possibly by his nephew, Prince Cuauhtémoc, cut short the emperor's conciliatory discourse and killed him. While the Aztec league was deliberating upon a successor, Cortés tried to lead his forces out of the city by night. He succeeded, but at the cost of heavy losses. At dawn he reviewed his shattered host, and, legend says, wept to see them in such a woeful state, with half of his soldiers floating, dead, on the waters of the lake. In history this is known as La Noche Triste (The Night of Sorrow).

On the way east, the Spaniards encountered an Aztec army, said by the chroniclers to have been 200,000 strong, a figure doubtless exaggerated. Cortés defeated it at Otumba, but again lost many men. He had left his cannon in Tenochtitlán and brought only a few horses, which having lost their novelty no longer frightened the Indians.

Cortés exhibited both patience and persistence. He took twelve months to build a flotilla and attack Tenochtitlán. The city was suffering from an epidemic of smallpox—caught from the Spaniards—and one of the victims was Cuitlahuac, Montezuma's successor. The 24-year-old Prince Cuauhtémoc then ascended the throne. The struggle for the city lasted eighty-five days; finally Cuauhtémoc was seized when he tried to flee, and in August, 1521, the city surrendered. The Spaniards did not find the treasure they had been led to expect. Rumor had it that Cuauhtémoc had flung it into the lake. Cortés tortured him in a vain attempt to make him tell where it was hidden, and some months later had him put to death.

Tenochtitlán had been half destroyed. Cortés ordered it rebuilt on the model of Spanish cities and kept it as the center of a series of expeditions to all points of the compass, in the course of which the Spaniards founded cities that are active and prosperous today—Guadalajara, Querétaro, Mérida, Morelia. This task took about twenty years, during which Cortés lived alternately in a palace he had built in Coyoacán, now a suburb of Mexico City, and in another, still standing, that he had built in Cuernavaca.

Cortés returned to Spain and dined at the table of Charles V, but he felt a longing for the lands he had conquered and returned to what was called the viceroyship of New Spain. There he found that, for all his titles and wealth, he had no power. He went back to Spain in 1540, and was allowed to take part, in a very limited capacity, in an expedition to Algiers, but by now he was an old man and he died soon afterward at the age of sixty-three, virtually forgotten.

Cortés had not only conquered Mexico but had discovered Lower California—sometime between 1535 and 1537. Now from the northern part of New Spain other expeditions set forth, usually with a small

number of men, and they explored New Mexico, Colorado, and central California. Meanwhile, an expedition, also from Mexico, explored and colonized Yucatán—where the descendants of the Mayas resisted for more than a century—and Guatemala.

The conquest was a mélange of cruelty, deceit, bravery, rash courage converging on madness, treachery, and many rivalries. For example, Cortés sent one of his captains to conquer Honduras. On the way, this captain declared himself independent and Cortés sent another captain to arrest him, but this envoy was captured. He pretended to ally himself to the rebel captain, and while they were at table, killed him.

But hand in hand with this brutality went religious fervor, which demanded that every expedition include friars. These men learned the local idioms and tried to convert the Indians. If they were not

successful, they baptized the natives en masse. They collected codices, gathered legends, and wrote chronicles; at the same time they ordered the pyramids destroyed and had churches built on their foundations.

The conquistadors were all ambitious to be rich; they redistributed the Indians' lands and the Indians to work them. They had women sent from Spain to become their wives, although they were quite accustomed to begetting children upon Indian girls. In the end they returned to Spain, with Indian servants and great wealth. But many could not readjust to the ceremonious and peaceful life of the old country; they missed the excitement of campaigns and the endless horizons of Mexico, and they went back to die, surrounded by their illegitimate children, who were, so to speak, the first Mexicans, the product of the enforced blending of the two races, the *mestizos*.

An illustration from the Duran codex shows the meeting of Cortés, the Aztec ambassador, and Doña Marina which took place on Good Friday, 1519.

For the moment, none of them supposed that they were establishing the basis of what would some day be an independent country. In accord with the concepts of the time, New Spain was the property of the Crown, and those who conquered it for the king received lands and men as their reward. But not all of them were willing to accept such a simple and sweeping arrangement.

Were the Indians human beings? Did Spain have the right to occupy the territories of other monarchs? These were questions some Spanish theologians asked themselves. Those who did not believe that the Indians were really human beings saw no obstacle to occupation of their lands. But those who did believe that the Indians were human (a belief shared by the Crown) used this as justification for the occupation of their kingdoms—they would convert them to Christianity.

The Church and the Crown had coinciding interests. The former wanted to make new Christians out of the Indians; the latter, new payers of taxes, perhaps new soldiers. Therefore it was necessary to protect them against the indifference and the greed of the conquistadors. This gave rise to two systems that were first applied to Mexico. First, there was the *encomienda,* by which a conquistador received a certain amount of land and the Indians who lived on it, in exchange for protecting and Christianizing them. The arrangement was in essence a transplant of the feudal system which had long since become moribund in Europe. To save the Indians from being entirely at the mercy of their new lords, and to preserve the ancient system of communal ownership, each Indian village was guaranteed a tract of common farm land—eventually standardized at one square league in size. These *ejidos,* as they were known, could not be sold; with these lands, waters, pastures, and woodlands, the Indians were able to subsist. The new lords, however, found ways to make the encomienda and the ejido profitable to themselves. The former gave them de facto dominion over the Indians; the latter enabled them to put the Indians to work on the conquistadors' lands without pay; since the natives could presumably live on the produce of their ejidos.

The Church soon saw the evil in this and brought pressure upon the Council for the Indies, seated in Seville, to have this legislation modified. The conquistadors rebelled against these new laws that restricted their "right" to dispose of the Indians as they pleased; they were willing to obey only the part that required them to supply labor for the mines, which were considered the property of the Crown and whose output of silver and gold went to finance the wars of Spain against the Protestants of Holland and Germany. Finally the conquistadors were victorious. Little by little, the Church lost her missionary zeal, and her role of protectress of the Indians was exchanged for that of a major proprietor of lands and peasants.

In resisting the Crown, the overseas Spaniards relied on the Castilian tradition of popular democracy. In Castile, in the Middle Ages, there was properly speaking no feudalism; rather, the common people were permitted a measure of democracy and freedom in return for their cooperation in fighting the Moors and populating the lands Spain reconquered. The holdovers from this tradition in the Americas were two institutions: the *cabildo,* or municipal council, with the *cabildo abierto,* an assembly of the people of the city, in which women also took part, and the *juicio de residencia,* according to which every functionary of the Crown, when his terms of office ended, had to remain for several weeks in the place where he had fulfilled his charge, to reply to any accusations that might be made against him. There were even some viceroys who, because of this custom, ended up in prison for abuses committed in office. But such institutions gradually lost importance; as time went on, the cabildos ceased to elect their officials (in some places the offices were sold) and the viceroys became responsible only to the king.

The conquistadors numbered only a few hundred and the first generation of colonists only a few thousand. How was it possible that three or four million Indians should resign themselves to domination by a mere handful of men? There are several explanations. For one thing, the different Indian peoples were leaderless; their chiefs and priests were dead, and as they knew nothing of democratic practices, when they lost their leaders they were left without any initiative. Furthermore, the Spaniards did not make their conquests unaided, but in alliance with Indian tribes who resented Aztec imperialism—which attitude, by the way, left no doubt in the minds of the conquistadors that the Indians were real human beings, no matter how their theologians might argue. Thirdly, the Aztec religion itself made it easier for its faithful to submit. Montezuma received Cortés with these

sant miguel capolapan

camino reca lapan

Hal tenas
camino Real De me Xico Valtepuc mas mas mas

santiago tonalapan.

tetela

plachepicahel

francisco Hotzopan

sancta maria es ump

sant pedro vertenilan

en San ŝua totutla

sant estevan quauhteno.

words, as recorded by an Indian chronicler: "Lord, you have striven,
you have wearied yourself, you have arrived at the land, at your city.
You have come here to occupy your throne. For a short time your
substitutes who have gone away, held it for you." In other words,
Montezuma believed that Cortés had come to regain Quetzalcoatl's
throne. In addition to all this, the Aztecs believed that the universe had
been destroyed four times: by flood, by fire, by earthquake, and by
wild beasts. The Spaniards were simply a fifth form of destruction, and
just as the sun, which dried up the waters after the fourth destruction,
demanded victims, the Spaniards were claiming workers for their lands.
Perhaps the Aztecs were surprised that they were not destroyed by the
Spaniards, and judged it better to submit than to be annihilated.

In any case, they did not immediately consent to give up their own
gods. In 1524 a group of Franciscan friars tried to convert several
Aztec astronomers and mathematicians. The sages, after hearing them
out, told the friars, according to an Aztec chronicle:

"We are common folk, mortals; then let us die, since our gods are
dead. You have said that we do not know the Lord of near and far,
the one who owns the heavens and the earth. . . . These are new sayings,
and we are troubled by them, for our ancestors, who are no more, did
not speak like this. They gave us their rules of life, they honored the
gods. We know to whom we owe birth, in which we ought to believe,
how to invoke the gods, how to pray."

But the friars built a Christian church above the ruins of every
pyramid, placed a saint's statue where each minor god had stood, a
statue of the Virgin in place of each goddess, and adapted their religion
to the Aztec rites: even Communion was recognized by the Aztecs, as
symbolic sacrifice such as they already celebrated.

It was therefore not difficult for them to change their religion. Still
less so when we know that the Indians continued their secret worship
of the former gods, whose images they hid in the foundations of the
roadway crosses and in the insides of the statues of the saints and
Christs they molded under the direction of the friars. More often than
not, when an image from the sixteenth century is accidently broken,
bits of an Aztec idol are found inside. Thus, the Indians, in adoring
the Virgin of Guadalupe, or Christ, or a saint, at the same time worshiped the memory of this or that god or goddess.

*A 1577 census map of a Tlaxcalan town in the Valley of Mexico shows the
typical colonial village organization of churches surrounded by adobe huts.*

In losing their own leaders, the Indians lost everything. The history of the three centuries of colonial life is the history of a long, silent recuperation, unconscious perhaps, but persistent. The number of Indians shrank greatly, by one account between 80 and 90 per cent, but the number of mestizos (children of unions of Spaniards and Indian women) rapidly increased. The skin color of the Indians grew lighter and that of the Spaniards grew darker.

At the end of a century—three generations of colonizers—it was no longer possible to speak of most of the inhabitants of New Spain as pure Indians or pure Spaniards. The Indians were found in certain regions, or on certain great haciendas, or in the mines; the Spaniards were in the government offices, or were officers of the army. Most of the population could be called Mexican, composed of mestizos and of Creoles—Spaniards born in Mexico. Both considered themselves rivals of the *peninsulares*—the Spaniards sent by the Crown to govern them. The history of the colony is, in great part, the history of this rivalry.

The struggle began with Bishop Bartolomé de las Casas, today venerated by the Mexicans as the apostle of the Indians. Las Casas spent his life traveling between New Spain and the mother country, where he succeeded in having various laws passed for the protection of the Indians. Repeatedly the Creoles rebelled against the viceroys, who were trying to enforce these laws, a struggle which persisted right into the eighteenth century in the form of opposition to all measures that the court of Madrid, then headed by the enlightened despot, Charles III, adopted to modernize the colonies. Along with these were other struggles: principally that of the Church against the civil authorities, at first on behalf of the Indians, but later, when the Church had become resigned to the status quo, over questions of precedence and ceremony. The Church had charge of all education, from primary school in churches and convents up to the university. Most of the famous Mexican writers of the colonial epoch were churchmen, and it was the Church that built cathedrals, monasteries, asylums, and hospitals. About twelve hundred religious edifices were built by the Indians under the direction of friars. The Indians also decorated the churches, and so created a special style, the Mexican baroque, a blending of Spanish techniques and Indian feeling and artistry. At the same time (though less relentlessly than in Spain) the Church persecuted

A Creole landlord in 1630 supervises the growing of cactus on his estate.
OVERLEAF: *A seventeenth-century view of teeming Plaza Mayor, Mexico City*

Semilla quese
yamadura ya
sacon para
gosto sep
tiembreyo
tubre avnque
todoelaño ay
cosecha pero
laprincipal
esenestosmese

VI.
Aquisecha po
daeltunal des
puesdehauerda
do yaelffruçto
ycogidosedela
cochinilladela
grana yestose
HaceporDici
embrey Hen
ro

heretics—certain Jews who had defied the royal prohibition and had settled in Monterrey, and Protestant pirates. For, although New Spain did not have any foreign wars, it had to face frequent attacks upon its coastal cities by English and French pirates. Fighting off these attacks, and the repression of various Indian uprisings (especially that of the Yaquis of Sonora and that of the descendants of the Mayas of Yucatán), constituted the only military activity in the three centuries of colonialism.

As this was the equivalent of a sentence of boredom for the soldiers, and afforded no chance for promotion, various exploring expeditions were organized, to the islands of Revilla Gigedo in the Pacific (named for the viceroy in whose term of office they were discovered) and to California, which was colonized by men under Gaspar de Portolá and converted by Fray Junípero Serra in the eighteenth century.

We must not lose sight of the fact that New Spain was much larger than present-day Mexico—it included the present American Southwest as well as all the area of present-day Central America north of Panama. But official life was concentrated in Mexico City, where the days were passed in constant preoccupation with ceremony and with the quarrels between the viceroy and the archbishops and between the viceroy and the Creoles. Except for this city and a few others on the plateau, and the very rich mines of Pachuca and Guanajuato, which produced a third of the world's silver, the land was entirely rural. Immense plantations, owned by the Creole descendants of colonizers and by monastic communities, spread over the parts of the country suitable for cultivation. Within each one were villages, ejidos, sometimes even a city. And the owners were defacto judges and governors through their agents.

New Spain was a stopping point between the mother country and the Philippines, from which Spain got her spices, silk, and ivory. The port of Acapulco, on the Pacific (now a tourist center but then a fever-ravaged village), awoke only twice a year, upon the arrival of the so-called Nao de China, the galleons that brought in the products of the Philippines. These goods were loaded on mules, long caravans of which crossed Mexico, up and across the plateau and down the valley to the Gulf Coast and the port of Veracruz, where the galleons that would take to Spain not only the products of the Pacific but also gold and silver bullion awaited. To prevent seizure of these treasure-laden ships by pirates, they were organized into fleets with the king's armada for escort. As a result of this system everything happened in six-month periods—each time mail came from Spain, with orders from the Council for the Indies for government officials, with news for the Creoles, and with European goods for those who could afford them.

There were not many people who fell into this last category. Aside from the high functionaries and several very wealthy families, the colonists relied on domestic products—food, home furnishings, and clothing. They were prohibited from producing some things, for Spain protected its own industries. Wine was one of the forbidden items. This partially accounts for the fact that Mexican wines, from grape-vines that are not very old, are not as good as those of Europe.

All Mexico's imports and exports had to pass through the port of Seville, and all trade had to be with Spain. All officials were sent from Spain instead of chosen from among people born in Mexico. Consequently the Creoles became increasingly antagonistic toward the court and the Council for the Indies. And, of course, the antagonism fed the very active smuggling trade, especially with the colonies in North America, and made smuggling a respectable and honorable profession. It was, really, a form of rebellion against Spanish colonialism. Nevertheless, the Creoles considered themselves loyal subjects of His Catholic Majesty the king of Spain. They never rebelled against him, but only against his officials.

Oddly enough, the same loyalty was to be found among the Indians. To them the king who promulgated laws and whom they had never seen (no Spanish monarch ever visited his American possessions) was a protector. The officials who collected taxes and ordered punishments, and the Creoles, who owned the lands and made the Indians work them, were the enemy. All the rebellions, whether Indian or Creole, echoed the cry "Long live the king and down with bad government."

Although none of these rebellions was a real danger to Spanish dominion, some were dramatic and some were picturesque. Even Cortés' son joined a conspiracy of conquistadors' sons against the viceroy who had persuaded Madrid to pass a law forbidding the handing down of encomiendas to the grandsons of conquistadors; the conspirators were discovered, and two were put to death, but Cortés' son escaped. In 1659 an Irishman in the viceroy's entourage, William

(Guillen de) Lamport, tried to have himself proclaimed viceroy by means of forged documents; he had a plan to then declare New Spain independent. He was burned at the stake by the Inquisition as a heretic, even though he was, to all appearances, insane.

A much more serious insurrection took place in 1761. It was set afoot by descendants of the Mayas under the leadership of one Jacinto Canek, who had been educated by the Church and spoke Latin. He had himself crowned emperor of the Mayas. After a three-month struggle he and eight of his lieutenants were seized and then drawn and quartered. A hundred of his followers had their right ears cut off.

In 1801 another Indian uprising broke out in Tepic, in the northwest near the Pacific coast. A king was proclaimed but the uprising was crushed. These Indian uprisings climaxed a series of local ones, most of them in the mines; they took place almost every generation and were always suppressed. There were also Negro rebellions. One was led by a powerful artisan, a slave named Yangas, who in 1609 succeeded in getting the authorities to grant him a measure of local autonomy, which he maintained until his death. These Negroes were descendants of the first slaves imported into New Spain several years after the conquest when the king authorized use of a slave force to replace the Indians killed in various colonies and to work the tropical lands along the Gulf. In Mexico proper, the native population was numerous and slaves were not needed except in Veracruz and the vicinity—and as a status symbol in the houses of rich city people. Hence, Mexico has never had a large Negro population.

The population of the country continued to change during the colonial epoch. The mestizos had increased considerably in number and had begun to assume minor administrative posts and to enter craft guilds; some became holders of small estates. Little by little, New Spain was being transformed into a mestizo country—which means that the conditions that were to give birth to modern Mexico were emerging.

The transformation was gradual and took place before anyone realized it. The first time the word "Mexico" was used to designate New Spain as a cultural and human entity and not merely as a colony was in the works of Mexican Jesuits who had moved to Italy after their order was expelled from all Spanish Crown territories in 1767. Perhaps these Jesuits, in speaking of Mexico, wanted to make trouble

L ECSMO · SEÑOR CONDE DE GALVES.

The popular Spanish viceroy, the Conde de Galvéz, is portrayed in a calligraphic style in a painting by Brother Pablo de Jesús done in 1796.

for the king who had persecuted them, but the fact that they chose this method and not another indicates a growing realization that Mexico was different, that despite the diversity of its people there were among all of them certain unifying common denominators: their desire for equality with the peninsulares, their special way of speaking Castilian, the fact that a large part of them were neither Indians nor whites but mestizos, and the mingling of the two cultures, Spanish and Indian, in their ways of feeling, acting, and thinking. Despite the cruelty of the encomienda system and the mother country's total exploitation of the colony's resources, Spain contributed to New Spain everything that she had evolved at home: her bureaucratic skill in governing efficiently and maintaining peace, by means of a governmental network that reached into even the most obscure corners, with twelve intendancies, three provincial courts, two courts of appeal, and an army of forty thousand men. Spain also contributed her culture, particularly through the Church, with 254 monastic communities and 1,073 local church groups, a university founded in 1553, and printing presses, the first of which was set up in 1534, less than fifteen years after Cortés' arrival. There were also botanic gardens, an academy of fine arts, a school of mining and engineering, and newspapers, with the daily *Gaceta de México,* founded in 1722, one of the earliest in the hemisphere.

Most of these achievements came long after the conquest. But as early as 1557, in Pachuca, one Bartolomé de Medina, had invented a process which was used for separating silver from ore by the use of mercury. And toward the end of the eighteenth century, a machine for taking the seeds out of cotton was invented, long before Whitney's gin; it was not used, for labor was so cheap that it was less expensive to pay peons (indentured laborers) to do such work than to build machines. This fact probably best symbolizes Mexico as a colony—cultural progress and social backwardness.

In 1803 the German Baron Alexander von Humboldt, on a trip around the world to make scientific observations, visited Mexico. He found the capital city one of the most spacious and most beautiful in the world, and one of the richest as well. Perhaps his impressions were colored by the fact that he enjoyed for three months the favors of a reigning beauty which he shared with the Venezuelan Simón Bolívar. This generous lady was not the only one in Mexico who lived like one

of the Merveilleuses of post-Revolutionary France. Mexico City had
become, in a way, the Paris of Middle America, but a Paris with a
social regime appropriate to an absolute monarchy.

The influence of the French Revolution was not limited to its effect
on customs. Despite the vigilance of the Inquisition, the works of the
French Encyclopedists entered the country, and the works of Voltaire
arrived to the delight of physicians, men of letters, lawyers, and
even some rationalist friars. In the small middle class, composed of
merchants and professional men, a liberal, anticlerical, and at times
anti-Hispanic outlook was forming. For this urban minority, Spain
was not only the country that forbade Creoles to hold government
posts and to trade with whomever they pleased, but also the country
that, in its fear of the French Revolution, was preventing the free
circulation of ideas.

And in the north the British colonies, less rich and less well ad-
ministered than New Spain, had won their independence and had
become the United States of America. Although traditionalist Catholics viewed the new liberal Protestant neighbor with distrust—it had at
that time a vaguely defined western frontier with New Spain—there
were some in Mexico who impatiently awaited the books and periodi-
cals smuggled from Boston, buying them at prices as high as those of
the silks and the British fabrics in which they were hidden.

In the legal and administrative sense, Mexico was a colony. But she
had enjoyed three centuries of peace while Spain was being bled white
on the battlefields of Europe. Mexico's people had created industries
and tilled the fields without any major setbacks, whereas in Spain
the expulsion of the Jews and Moors, emigration to the Americas,
and wars had set the economy on a downward path.

Furthermore, Mexico was richer, better ordered, more cultivated,
and more prosperous than the mother country. If one forgot the darker
skin of the majority of the population and some pre-Cortés survivals
of custom, Mexico was what Spain might have been if she had not
become embroiled in the quarrels of the Old World. Spain had tried to
create another Spain, a new one, in America. Without realizing it, she
had created a Spain so new that it turned out to be Mexico. Growing
numbers of Creoles and mestizos had become aware of the situation,
and events in Spain were to move this minority from words to deeds.

CHAPTER III

EXIT
THE VICEROYS

When France and England resumed hostilities in 1803, a chain of events began which were to cause profound disturbances as far away as Mexico and the New World. Spain was drawn into the contest on France's side. England built up alliances against Napoleon and the French emperor tried to impose his Continental System by which Europe's commerce with England would be blockaded; three ports in the Iberian Peninsula—Lisbon, Cádiz, and Barcelona—were closed to English trade. Napoleon and Charles IV of Spain signed an agreement to divide Portugal, England's ally, and in furtherance of their objective, Madrid consented to the passage of French troops across Spanish territory. Napoleon's intent was not merely to occupy Portugal, but to seize the entire peninsula—or, at least, this entered his mind by the time his troops were in Spain.

Napoleon hastened the moment by intriguing with Charles' son, Ferdinand, promising the heir apparent support in his drive to take over the Spanish throne. When the royal squabble broke out in the open, French troops crossed the border, their mission ostensibly to help settle the affair. Charles was forced to abdicate in favor of Ferdinand.

Rivera here portrays the principals of the War of Independence: a balding Father Hidalgo flanked by Morelos on his left and Allende on his right.

This gave Napoleon the opening he needed. Promising to recognize Ferdinand as king, he lured him to Bayonne, where Charles IV was also awaiting the emperor's pleasure, and there both father and son yielded in favor of Joseph Bonaparte, Napoleon's brother. Although many highly placed Spanish officials went over to Joseph Bonaparte, the masses—led by a number of regional revolutionary juntas—were opposed; and this marked the beginning of a popular war, called by the Spanish the War of Independence, that was to last five years.

The news of Spain's invasion by the French, of Bonaparte's illegal seizure of the throne, and of the popular risings against him, reached Spanish America in the summer of 1808. Here, too, men were forced to reconsider where their allegiance lay. Independence was the issue and the opportunity.

The kingdoms of the New World—this of course included Mexico —had never belonged to Spain. Rather they were the patrimony of the Crown of Castile, and later, of the rulers of a united Spain, a legalistic distinction which custom had tended to obliterate but which at this moment of imperial crisis suddenly had real significance. Now with Ferdinand, the true king, held prisoner in France, there was no longer any legitimate authority to bind the colonies to Spain. The juntas by now had been superseded by one central junta, and it argued that in Ferdinand's absence it would rule in his name. Perhaps anticipating trouble with the colonies but also for philosophical reasons, it issued a royal decree recognizing equal rights for Spaniards and Hispano-Americans alike and ordered that representatives of Spain's overseas dominions be seated in the Cortes. The body went on to declare that "From this moment, Spanish Americans, you see yourselves free men. . . . Your destinies no longer depend on ministers, viceroys or governors; they are in your hands."

These seemingly generous words and the political situation implicit in them—direct ties with the Spanish nation under a common liberal constitution—reinvigorated the old feud between Creoles and peninsulares. Each group sought to gain the upper hand with the viceroy by forming unnatural alliances with powers in Spain. The peninsulares (or *gachupines,* as they were derogatorily called by the Creoles), who filled most of the important administrative posts in Mexico but who were numerically weak, came out in favor of the junta. Not that they were liberal, but they regarded the tentative steps toward autonomy being offered by the junta as a means of stalling while efforts were made to reinstate Ferdinand and the old order.

But the Creoles who had long been restive under what was in effect the peninsulares' oligarchic rule refused to recognize the sovereignty of the junta. They swore allegiance to the king's person—and to his appointed viceroy Iturrigaray—but not to some self-constituted body of Spaniards pretending to represent him but really representing the very Spanish aristocracy they resented.

The crisis came to a head on September 15, 1808, after Mexico City's cabildo, representing the Creoles, and its *audencia,* or high court, representing the peninsulares, failed to agree on the responsibilities of the viceroy under the new regime. A small group of peninsulares seized Iturrigaray, deported him, and put a pro-junta man in his place. When he proved too weak to maintain the coup, a succession of other pro-peninsulare, pro-junta viceroys took his place. In Mexico City Creole opposition was suppressed but in the countryside active conspiracy gained force and though most were discovered and many arrests made, one conspiracy was not exposed in time to head it off.

Its center was the city of Querétaro, and its prime mover was Don Ignacio de Allende, a Creole who had been an army captain. Another of the conspirators was Miguel Hidalgo y Costilla, a 57-year-old parish priest of the village of Dolores, who had some Enlightenment leanings and strong loyalties among his Indian flock. In September, 1810, the conspirators learned that they had been denounced. Several of them met in Dolores and decided to stage a coup. With no time to organize a rebellion among the Creoles and the army, they looked to the Indians for support. They arrested all the wealthy Spaniards in the town and the next day, Sunday, the sixteenth of September, Hidalgo preached to his Indian congregation against submission to Spain and ended with the battle cry that came to be called the "Grito de Dolores": "Long live Ferdinand VII! Long live Our Lady of Guadalupe! Down with the gachupines!" It was the beginning of five years of civil war.

The conspirators, now in arms, set out for Guanajuato, the great silver mining center, and on the way picked up many followers among the farm laborers they met. Once in Guanajuato, Hidalgo proclaimed himself general and Allende lieutenant general. The Spaniards and

The blending of the races is treated in this series of genre scenes by an anonymous colonial artist. Each picture theoretically represents one of the dozens of ethnic couplings and progeny possible in Mexico. The conjugations shown are in the archaic nomenclature of the time. Left, top to bottom,

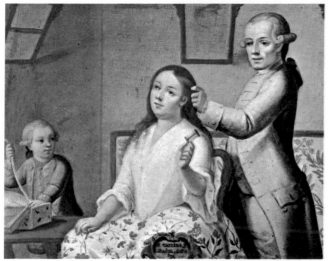

an Española and a Negro produced a Mulata; Mestizo and Española—Castiza; Mulata and Barquino—Coyote. Right, top to bottom, India and Lobo produced Sambaigo; Castiza and Español—Español; Torna Altras and Indio—Lobo. Finally all persons of mixed blood were called mestizos.

the authorities took refuge in the Alhondiga (the communal grain warehouse), but Hidalgo, with a group of miners, captured the warehouse and the city, massacring the gachupines as they went. A month later, with much of northern Mexico theirs, the rebel leaders occupied the city of Valladolid—present-day Morelia. There they published decrees abolishing slavery and the paying of taxes and tribute by Indians and Negroes. The rebels' strength was in the lower classes and this made it essential to take note of their aspirations. Thus the revolution for independence became a class war.

The two government regiments went over to Hidalgo and he marched on the capital, first sending in one of his partisans, José María Morelos, to organize an army in the territory between Acapulco and Cuernavaca. Near the capital, Hidalgo defeated the Spanish troops— there were not more than 1,300—but did not try to take the city because the popular uprising on which he had counted had not occurred. This was a fatal mistake, for it gave the viceroy time to recruit more forces. On the seventh of November, 7,000 men commanded by the viceroy confronted Hidalgo's 40,000 hastily collected and undisciplined followers and defeated them. Meanwhile, Allende and some of the other military leaders of the rebellion had begun to show signs of disenchantment, for Hidalgo's zealous work on behalf of the Indians was causing conflict with Creole interests. Hidalgo sought to hold the Creoles by offering them positions of rank in the movement, but he was now rapidly losing ground.

Learning that his forces had taken Guadalajara, Hidalgo went to that city and set up a government. There his Guadalajara Manifesto abolished taxes and tributes imposed on mestizos and Negroes, forbade slavery, and ordered the return of their land to the Indian villages (that is, the reconstitution of the ejidos which the landholding Creoles had been illegally appropriating). Then he sent an ambassador to the United States to form an alliance, but the envoy never reached his destination, for he was seized on the way by the Spaniards.

The insurgents decided to march to the United States, hoping to raise support against the Spaniards and to regroup their forces there. But they were betrayed and were arrested in March, 1811. Hidalgo was tried by the Inquisition and was condemned to death by firing squad. Allende and his lieutenants were also shot.

Although Hidalgo, excommunicated by the Church, had recanted in his last moments, in Mexico he is considered the father of his country. But in reality, the man who brought about independence was Morelos. Like Hidalgo, he was a parish priest, the son of a carpenter. When Hidalgo rebelled, Morelos rushed off to the Sierra at the head of twenty-five men from his parish. Several hacienda owners and their peasants joined him. After Hidalgo was executed, Morelos' guerrillas were the only force left to fight for independence. Though the Spaniards may have thought that their troubles were over, there was now more disorganized unrest than ever. Morelos' men won several important battles, and occupied Taxco, Cuautla, Oaxaca, Acapulco, and eventually all of southern Mexico save Mexico City, Puebla, and Veracruz. With the revolution once again vigorous, Morelos called a congress which met in Chilpancingo in September, 1813, and there he expounded his concept of the proper organization of an independent Mexican nation: it was to be Catholic, a republic governed democratically with three separate powers; it was to exclude immigrants who were not artisans, to try to establish equality of its citizens, to combat poverty through redistribution of land and confiscation of the wealthy class' property, and to prevent the concentration of wealth in the hands of a few. It should recognize free trade, respect private property, and substitute a general income tax for all other taxation. Obviously Morelos, who may have read the works of Thomas Paine, had ideas that for his epoch and for Mexico were modern and advanced. Like Hidalgo, he condemned slavery and the levying of tribute upon Indians and Negroes.

While the congress was debating the new constitution, Morelos continued to fight on. (It is interesting to note how Morelos' battlefield covered the same territory that, a century later, would be the center of the agrarian revolution.) Morelos relied on the landless peasants, who hoped to receive lands from the new independent authorities and who, still landless a hundred years later, would again rise in armed rebellion.

The congress proclaimed the independence of Mexico and in 1814 issued the first constitution of the new country. About this time Ferdinand VII returned to the Spanish throne and many moderates consequently lost interest in Mexico's revolt. Already there were many signs

OVERLEAF: *A cross section of nineteenth-century Mexican society can be seen viewing a procession of sacred statues during a Holy Week celebration.*

of disunity, and the congress, more moderate than the fighters for independence, whose aspirations Morelos had expressed, accepted Morelos' political ideas but not his social ones. Significantly, it introduced no changes in the fiscal system or in the ownership of land.

Meanwhile, Morelos' military victories had alarmed the royalists, and they deposed the viceroy and replaced him by a military man. From that time Morelos' forces rapidly lost ground and the rebel government perforce became a wandering one. In these struggles a Creole officer, Agustín de Iturbide, distinguished himself, winning several victories for the royalists. When Morelos' forces were routed at the revolutionary center of Valladolid the movement was severely disrupted. Morelos was soon captured and hauled off to Mexico City. There the Inquisition defrocked him, degraded him, and he was shot by the civil authorities in December, 1815.

However, Morelos' death did not end the struggle; guerrillas he had organized carried it on. What happened in Mexico was the same thing that had happened in Spain during the war against Napoleon—the people organized as guerrillas, and kept the regular army at bay, preventing it from dominating the territory, but failing to win a decisive victory themselves.

By 1819, four years after the execution of Morelos, only about eight thousand guerrillas were left to face the royalist troops. The old leaders were either dead or disenchanted. Idealism had given way to the personal ambitions of local chiefs. The independent government had become disunited; many of its proponents had taken advantage of an amnesty offered by the viceroy. On the field of battle only one of Morelos' lieutenants was left, Vicente Guerrero. (There are several states and cities whose names pay tribute to the admiration the Mexicans felt for the insurgents: the states of Hidalgo and Guerrero, and the city of Morelia among them.) Although Guerrero had nearly always been defeated, he was able to maintain a guerrilla force strong enough to strike constantly at the royalists. He received an unexpected reinforcement in 1817 with the arrival in Mexico of the famous Spanish guerrilla fighter, Francisco Javier Mina, who had fought the French in his country, had been imprisoned in Paris, and at the end of the War of Independence had conspired with the liberals against the absolutism of Ferdinand. Exiled to London, Mina rounded up the money to organize an expedition in aid of the Mexican insurgents. In Baltimore, he collected more money, arms, and four ships. He disembarked on the Mexican Gulf Coast and won several resounding victories, but was captured and executed. His brief presence nevertheless gave new heart to the insurgents, although they had been somewhat distrustful of him because he was not fighting against Spain but only against the absolutism of the Spanish king.

Ferdinand's actions had a major influence on Mexico's decision to be independent. When the "Desired One" was restored to Spain in 1814, he immediately showed himself to be an absolutist and he abolished the new Cádiz constitution. He then set out to re-establish the prewar machinery of government and to suppress all opposition. By 1820, when the insurrection in Mexico had almost spent itself, unrest in the mother country had reached the explosive point again; a Spanish commander, Rafael del Riego, staged a military coup against Ferdinand. He was backed by the troops collected to embark for America to fight the insurgents in South America—a war for independence had broken out in Argentina and Venezuela and the Spanish had fared worse than in Mexico. The military coup compelled Ferdinand to accept the constitution of Cádiz and to reinstate parliament.

Although freedom of the press had lasted only two months in the Mexican colony, for the viceroy had immediately suppressed the newspapers founded to take advantage of it, those two months were a time of much forceful writing about the evils of colonial administration and about the Church. They were enough to make the journalistic fame of José Joaquín Fernández de Lizardi, who in 1812 founded the newspaper *El Pensador Mexicano* (The Mexican Thinker) and who wrote a very harsh satire on colonial life in the form of a novel, *El Periquillo Sarniento* (which has been translated into English as *The Itching Parrot*).

In Mexico, this reinstatement of the Cádiz constitution with its liberal, anticlerical bias, sent conservatives and the Church into action. They decided on a secession of their own, for only independence would insure the maintenance of the old order. They sought an alliance with the heirs of their former enemy Morelos, whose remaining forces were now led by Guerrero. The man chosen to lead the combined forces was Agustín de Iturbide.

Iturbide was regarded as a conservative. He was presently unoccupied, for he had been cashiered from the army when it was revealed that he had been taking protection money from the owners of the mine whose envoys he was detailed to escort. The choice of this man as negotiator with the insurgents was made by a group of conservatives who met secretly in the Profesa convent in the capital. They persuaded the unsuspecting viceroy that Iturbide should be returned to the field to conquer Guerrero's insurgents; in reality, Iturbide sought reconciliation with the rebels. Afterward, Iturbide would present himself as the inspirer of the entire plot, but actually he was only the temporary instrument of the Machiavellian scheming of some frightened clerics and bureaucrats.

The insurgents were not inclined to like Iturbide because he had put himself at the services of the royalists and also because he had shown himself to be a cruel and implacable fighter against Morelos. Moreover he had taken advantage of the general disorder to advance his own fortunes. The viceroy appointed Iturbide commander of the troops fighting the remnants of Guerrero's war-weary forces in the south. He met with the latter and proposed that they form a common movement to make Mexico independent. Guerrero was suspicious, but he was in a difficult situation. They conferred at Iguala, and Guerrero agreed to subordinate himself to Iturbide. Then in February, 1821, Iturbide drafted the so-called Plan de Iguala (a *plan*, in the history of Mexico, is any manifesto or program announced publicly by an individual or organization in rebellion against the incumbent administration). This plan was read to Iturbide's and Guerrero's troops, who swore to uphold it in March, 1821. It advocated independence, a constitutional monarchy, Catholicism as the official religion, racial equality, and the protection of private property. Finally, it proposed the formation of an army that would be called triguarantor—that is, that would guarantee independence, the Catholic religion, and the union of Creoles and Europeans. This triple guarantee was symbolized in the tricolor flag that was to be adopted for the new country: white symbolizing the purity of religion, red signifying union, and green standing for independence. It is obvious that with this plan Iturbide was making sure that nothing in the social order should be upset and that political change would be limited to a change of monarchy. The insurgents

José María Morelos, once a mestizo parish priest, and later the martyred leader of the independence movement, is portrayed by an anonymous artist.

accepted the plan because they wanted independence above all else and despaired of winning it by themselves.

The Iguala Plan also impressed the Creoles of the various provinces of Guatemala (subsequently divided into the five Central American republics of Guatemala, Honduras, El Salvador, Nicaragua, and Costa Rica) and each separately declared independence too. Realizing that they were small and therefore defenseless, they agreed to ask Iturbide's government to annex them.

Iturbide's only opposition was a group of royalist officers who considered the viceroy's failure to consult them as a betrayal. Deposing the king's regent, they placed one of their number in his stead, prepared to join the struggle in an attempt to halt the advance of the triguarantor army. Meanwhile, Spain sent a new viceroy who entered into negotiations with Iturbide, and in August, 1821, signed the Treaty of Córdoba, in the city of that name, near Veracruz. The viceroy did not go beyond hoping that Ferdinand or one of his Bourbon relatives would be named ruler of Mexico. In September, Iturbide, at the head of a sixteen-thousand-man army, made his triumphal entry into the capital.

A provisional junta was then formed. It consisted of thirty-eight members, among them Iturbide, the viceroy himself, many royalists, some Creoles, and a few insurgents, and was to have the task of choosing the ruler of the new country.

Mexico was now independent—at least in theory. But many regarded this independence as factitious, since the insurgents did not so much want to liberate themselves from Spain (which was far away and had now become liberal) as from the Spanish functionaries and aristocrats who had governed New Spain and had closed all doors to the Creoles. But it became evident that these same elements were again going to govern, this time in the name of independence, and that they would also be the ones who would name the future Mexican sovereign.

The provisional junta drafted an Act of Independence, convoked a constituent congress, and appointed a regency of five members, headed by Iturbide. In the congress, the members of which were elected as representatives of *estamentos,* or the social classes, as if it were a medieval parliament, three parties emerged: the Bourbonists, who wanted to put a Bourbon on the throne; the Iturbidistas, who wanted

Don Miguel Hidalgo is shown sitting in his study. In 1810 he led an uprising in Dolores on September 16, a date celebrated annually as Independence Day.

to make the Generalissimo king; and the republicans, who did not want any king at all.

The Bourbonists were placed in an awkward situation when the Spanish government refused to acknowledge the independence of Mexico, for this automatically eliminated any candidacy by a Bourbon. It was not known whether they would resign themselves to the idea of a republic or give their votes to Iturbide. The latter had no intention of waiting to find out. In May, 1822, a sergeant incited his comrades in arms to proclaim Iturbide emperor. A group of them met and marched through the streets, gathering the people of the city along with them and shouting, *"Viva Agustín!"* Congress met next day and by a vote of 67 to 15, with 74 abstentions, proclaimed Iturbide emperor of Mexico with the title Agustín I. Two months later he was crowned with pomp and ceremony to match the royal houses of Europe.

That was the only tranquil moment of his reign. The exchequer was nearly empty, salaries were owed to the troops, and in distributing high posts and honors, the government had satisfied only the wealthy Creoles. The republicans began to conspire, and since a lot of them were insurgents of 1810 and many had fought in the guerrilla wars, the danger of civil overthrow was by no means imaginary. Many arrests were made, including fifteen deputies, Guerrero among them.

Between congress and the emperor there were almost daily conflicts now over the deputies' desire to maintain their legislative freedom and to limit the powers of the sovereign. Agustín, to put an end to the disputes, sent a battalion to dissolve the body by force in October, 1822, hardly three months after his coronation.

Although his army carried out the directive, it was by no means united. Some of its commanders had been in the royalist forces; others had been insurgents. One of the former, Antonio López de Santa Anna, was disappointed over Iturbide's failure to grant him career advancement. Seeking revenge, he led his forces in a rebellion at Veracruz. Some weeks later Guerrero and other former insurgents escaped from prison.

Guerrero sent a force in pursuit of Santa Anna, but instead of attacking him, they signed a manifesto demanding restoration of the congress. His generals having aligned themselves with Santa Anna, Iturbide consented; twelve days after the congress met again he presented his abdication, for he had been disheartened to find the imperial career less easy and brilliant than he had imagined. He had been used to the absolutism of the viceroy's rule and could not adapt himself to a democratic government (however defective the new Mexican democracy may have been) in which his desires were not taken as orders, nor his orders enforced by the army.

Iturbide's fall marked the beginning of Santa Anna's political career. Here was a personality who was to appear intermittently on the Mexican scene for almost half a century and who would be to Mexico's history like the chili pepper is to its cooking.

Congress did not accept the abdication of Agustín I, preferring to declare that his coronation had been obtained under duress and so was invalid. Iturbide left with his family for Italy; only eight months had elapsed since his coronation. So that he might not feel any temptation to return, the congress voted him a stipend of 25,000 pesos a year, a considerable sum in those days, for as long as he remained in Italy.

However, there was not to be any simple solution to the country's affairs. Congress appointed a military triumvirate, composed of insurgents who differed as to whether there should be a federation or a centralist state. The centralist insurgents, the more moderate faction, sought the support of former Bourbonists and Iturbidists, which meant that ex-royalists would continue to influence the government of the new country.

Another difficulty was that Iturbide had proved a poor administrator, and that there was no money available to pay the army and the bureaucrats. The latter, most of whom had been employed under the viceroy, began to mutter that when Mexico had been New Spain this sort of thing had never happened, and that they had always been paid on time.

Moreover, the Central American provinces, which had joined Mexico, decided to secede when Iturbide fell, for they feared being caught up in the inner struggles they foresaw for Mexico. The Mexican government sent a force of five thousand men, but their general realized that the provinces' desire to separate was genuine, and decided to withdraw. The five provinces proceeded to form a new country, the United Provinces of Central America, which for twenty years would be the scene of civil quarrels and wars.

Meanwhile, in Mexico, a new constituent congress was elected in November, 1823. The decisions to be made were major. How was the new country to be organized—as a federal or centralist state? What were to be the relations of Church and State? Decisions had to be made about Spanish and Indian property, about international policy for the future, and especially about relations with its powerful neighbor, the United States, and about the relative influence of the different classes of society in the process of decision-making itself.

None of this was going to be simple, for many interests were involved. Furthermore, until then the Mexicans had never been participants in formulating policies affecting their lives; the Indians had not done so under the Aztec emperors, nor had the colonists under the viceroys. In short, there had been no training in this difficult art. It was not enough for the law to declare that there would be elections. How were the mass of the people to be interested in political questions? How were they to be informed, and given such criteria that they might vote with at least a minimum of rationality? In short, how were these former subjects to be taught to convert themselves into citizens? Furthermore, institutions and even the people's way of thinking had to be transformed. How was an Indian to be told that he was no longer to look to a distant king for justice, but to a president who was closer at hand? How were the Creoles to be made accustomed to the newly acquired freedom of speech, of organization, and of trade? How were people to be taught not to consider the president a mere substitute for the viceroy on whose head they might discharge all their frustrations and discontents? The congress drafted a constitution of the federal type, inspired by that of the United States, though distinctly Mexican in its legalization of the Catholic Church. The federal republic was to consist of nineteen states and four territories, with each state electing its own governor and legislature. The nineteen legislatures would in turn select the president and vice-president. Regarding the allocating of power—legislative, judicial, and executive—in government, the example of the American system was again followed.

For three centuries the viceroys had concentrated in their own hands all three branches, and this tradition carried such weight that when Morelos had organized the first independentist congress, that body assumed all three roles itself. General Guadalupe Victoria, whose

Iturbide's Army of the Three Guarantees, shown here entering Mexico City, promised Catholicism, a constitutional monarchy, and equality for all.

adopted name—signifying Our Lady of Guadalupe Triumphant— was borrowed from the battle cry of the first Hidalgo-Morelos insurgents, was chosen the first president and began his term late in 1824. The general was a national hero, having fought an uncompromising guerrilla campaign against Spain and Iturbide for many years. It was not the best preparation for the sensitive new post he was chosen to fill.

Meanwhile, the exiled Iturbide had been flattered into thinking that he still had sufficient support in Mexico to seize back his throne. It was also rumored that Spain was plotting another invasion. With high expectations of a triumphal return he set sail for Mexico once more. He was falling into a trap, however, for his supporters in a last desperate effort to hold their waning power had vastly overstated the situation. When Iturbide landed he found himself branded "a traitor and an outlaw" and he was captured and shot shortly after landing, on July 19, 1824. With this Mexico can be considered to be truly independent. From this moment the Spanish ceased to exert any direct influence and the Mexicans began to make their own decisions.

The nation which the inexperienced Guadalupe Victoria and his government were entrusted to lead was in a parlous condition. The land was rich in appearance only. There were a few extremely wealthy Mexicans and a great number of extremely poor ones, and between them only a small middle class. Moreover, the very sources of wealth had suffered from the long war. Agriculture had lost part of its work force and many fields had been laid waste. What little industry there was acted with caution; if it was true that one could now hope for world trade, there was no assurance of a market for domestic products; merchants and industrialists had never sold abroad, for Spanish law forbade it. The mines had not been modernized in many years; there was no money to buy new machinery, and Mexican metals had lost their only customer, Spain. The Church virtually owned nearly all the available money. There were no banks and the credit was in the hands of the Church. Thus the civil power faced an economy mediated by the Church—and the Church had not been favorable to the idea of independence.

Not only did most of the Spaniards in the country return home, leaving the country without experienced major officials, but a lot of the native rich emigrated too, at least temporarily, fearful of unstable

conditions, and took their fortunes along. It would have been possible,
certainly, to have recourse to foreign capital, but as the colony had
been accustomed to receiving money only from Spain, there was no
experience in international financial relations. Yet it was essential to
pay the army and the bureaucrats, at a time when the easy, fatal, and
catastrophic recourse of printing money was not available, for all the
colony's money had been of silver and gold, and independent Mexico
could not commence its career by substituting bits of paper for the
precious metals.

People who had a minimum of Western culture and education,
meaning the small middle class, were beginning to show a great curi-
osity about the rest of the world. Facts and concepts had to be assimi-
lated by minds unaccustomed to thinking for themselves or to express-
ing their ideas. The Church and the authorities had lost their monopoly
over thought. And a taste of intellectual freedom only bred still greater
impatience to discover everything at once.

All these things, coming at the same time, were to give a chaotic and
troubled quality to the early years of independence. This history of the
first half century of Mexico's freedom is precisely the history of efforts
to give coherence to agitated aspirations. The people would need fifty
years of apprenticeship to turn them into citizens and to make the land
into a nation, and that half century was to decide what purposes were
to be served by the independence they had desired.

CHAPTER IV

THE FIFTY-YEAR
APPRENTICESHIP

T he nearly five decades between Iturbide's execution in 1824 and
the ouster of Maximilian in 1867 carried Mexico from the first stages
of nationhood to its maturity. The era is a mixture of the heroic and the
grotesque, the dramatic and the comic, the romantic and the cynical.
The physical aspect of the country itself was to change very little. In
the rural areas, the villages were still composed of adobe huts and a
stone church; the hacienda compounds were laid out with broad dwellings sheltered from the heat by thick walls, a chapel for the *señores*
and an open atrium for the laborers, and storage sheds for corn, coffee,
beans, and rice. New crops, restricted during the colonial years because
of competition with Spanish imports, were cultivated; vineyards were
planted, and cattle raising was increased to meet the demand for more
meat in the cities. Meat, however, was found only on the tables of the
well to do, for the mass of people maintained their traditional impoverished diet of rice, beans, and corn in various forms, including *tor-
tillas*. The peasants continued to wear a style of dress little altered by
three centuries—cotton trousers or skirts, and blouses. Industrial workers adopted the black shirt as their informal uniform.

*In this mural by Diego Rivera, two victims of the Mexican Inquisition become
symbols of the centuries-long repression of the common people.*

In the haciendas and in the town houses of the señores there were many servants. Vendors paraded every morning through the unpaved streets of towns and cities. The de luxe shops were usually French, the food stores Spanish. Mining was in a state of decay. Travel was by stagecoach or on horseback over roads poorly kept up. The authorities were so constantly involved in internecine struggles that they had little time left for public service. The bureaucracy was growing, to form an eternally discontented group at once stable and fearful.

However, the inner struggles and foreign wars directly affected only a minority of Mexicans. The armies numbered just a few thousand men, the battles caused relatively little damage, and people went on leading routine lives without troubling themselves overmuch about the cannon booming a few miles from their homes.

Little by little, European and North American styles of life were beginning to invade the rich, urban parts of the country. There were newspapers in the capital and in various provincial cities. The number of private schools—religious and some foreign—was increasing. Special schools were established (technical, medical), and as time went on the university became more up-to-date.

The government derived its funds chiefly from customs tariffs, and from indirect taxes. When it was short of money, which was much of the time, it floated loans from private banks, generally British, for Great Britain had made good relations with Mexico a pillar of its policy of containing the United States in Spanish America. As long as the brief periods of peace lasted, people were able to live in security, though in the open countryside banditry was rife and travel from place to place continually hazardous. It was always wise to move in caravans.

It is remarkable that in such a troubled half century there was quasi-modernization. Telegraph lines were strung; textile mills were built and machinery was imported for them. The postal service operated, Spanish dramatic and zarzuela troupes made frequent visits, and cultural novelties from Europe and the United States gave educated Mexicans the illusion that they were citizens of the world.

Little by little capital accumulated, some Mexican banks were established, factories were built, the mines were restored to operation. Wealthy women could shop for the latest Paris fashions and men could buy the latest books from Madrid and Barcelona. It might be said that there were two countries in Mexico: that of the well to do who lived in European style and cultivated Continental tastes, attempted to obtain titles—if not from the king of Spain, at least from the Vatican—dazzled Europeans when they traveled to Paris and London, voted and stood for election, and did the governing. The other Mexico was that of the artisans, the first factory workers, and the peasants who lived like serfs on the haciendas, almost wholly illiterate; none of them voted, or were candidates, or had any idea who was governing them; and they dressed, ate, and thought in a way entirely different from that of the middle class and the señores. These two countries brushed shoulders and made a sort of half-acquaintance only when there were political events of the kind that aroused strong emotions. When that happened, the politicians and military men of wealthy Mexico sought soldiers from the Mexico of the poor.

These struggles, changes of government, civil wars, intrigues, military coups, and rebellions took place in the capital and in the states of the central plateau. There was hardly any activity on the coasts, either political or economic, for these regions were inhospitable places where yellow fever and a sultry climate prevailed. Visitors stayed in the ports (especially Veracruz) just long enough to take ship or disembark and made haste to go up to the fresher and more healthful resorts in the Sierra. In the *llanuras* (plains) of the north there was little economic life and no political life at all; at the time when Mexico won her independence, this region included today's American Southwest.

Very soon in the life of the new country, after the initial enthusiasm of success had worn off, the various ideologies which had prompted the revolt from Spain became polarized. Those men who aligned themselves with the first insurgents were liberalists and federalists; the independentists of Iturbide's group were conservative and centralist. One might say that, as one went from left to right, the skin color lightened; most of the liberals were rural-minded mestizos, while the majority of the conservatives were urban Creole or Spanish, a homogeneous group of better-educated, more prosperous people drawn from the upper-class landowners, the Church, and the military. But the great mass of the people played no part whatever in politics—an affair of the cities, limited to people of some means and education. The capital tended to be conservative; the cities of the provinces were liberal; the

rural areas when they took notice at all leaned toward whomever the *hacendado,* or local strong man, favored. It should be understood that, in order to vote, a man had not only to know how to read and write but also had to own a minimum of property. In this Mexico imitated the system prevalent in Europe.

Meanwhile, the conflict between liberals and conservatives was fueled by the rise of Freemasonry in Mexico. The movement, which had been born and propagated in eighteenth-century England, had its adherents all over Europe and had made its way to Mexico in 1813. In its British manifestation it had been an apolitical, deistic, and essentially social organization of concerned gentlemen. But in its Continental incarnations it evolved into an active political, anticlerical force, the spearhead of rational liberal reform activities. Mexico's Freemasons had split into two factions, superficially based upon their allegiance to either the Scottish Rite or York Rite Lodge of the mother country, but the choice of rite became a matter of political persuasion. The conservative-centralists, including Vice-President Nicolás Bravo, joined the Scottish Rite, or Escoceses; the liberal-federalists, including President Guadalupe Victoria and the constitutional leader Miguel Ramós Arispe, ascribed to the Yorkino group.

The genteel manners of the provincial upper classes are evident in this painting of an 1844 banquet in honor of the governor of Oaxaca.

At the very commencement of her history as an independent country, Mexico was caught between two rival foreign forces as well. On one side were the European countries belonging to the Holy Alliance, who wanted to establish monarchies in the former colonies, and on the other, the United States, which wanted to fortify the republican regimes. In both instances, they also sought large trade concessions.

When the American envoy, Joel R. Poinsett, sent by President John Quincy Adams to secure trade privileges in Mexico, began distributing charters for York Rite Lodge, he ran headlong into Britain's commercial envoy and Scottish Ritist H. G. Ward, and the strains increased. The rivalries broke out into the open when the English bankers who had extended Victoria's government a sizable loan went into bankruptcy before Mexico had received all its money. The Yorkinos suspended the payment of the existing national debt and the Escoceces thought they saw in the disorder their opportunity to seize power. The abortive attempt only succeeded in having their leader, Bravo, exiled, and in turning popular favor toward the Yorkinos once again.

Victoria managed to include in his government elements of both political leanings. Thus Lucas Alamán, who belonged to the Scottish Rite and was a friend of the British envoy, had the portfolio of foreign affairs, and Lorenzo de Zavala, a Yorkist lodge member and friend of Poinsett, was finance minister. Zavala was criticized by those who opposed the protectionist policy he followed to provide revenue and to help artisans and budding industries. Both men later wrote histories of Mexico that are at once documents of their times and excellent literary works. And both played decisive roles in the events of their day.

Elections were held in 1828. The provincial legislatures chose a moderate non-Mason, Manuel Gómez Pedraza, who ran against the old insurgent Vicente Guerrero. The latter's supporters were not resigned to his defeat, and Santa Anna, who had rebelled against Iturbide, now rebelled again. He issued another Plan, which declared the election invalid and Guerrero the rightful president. This, and a liberalist riot in the capital, persuaded the congress to annul the election and, in the first of a long series of unconstitutional acts, to choose Guerrero. Pedraza fled the country.

During his nine months in power, Guerrero had to fight off a plot hatched by the Spanish king and members of Mexico's conservative wing; its object was to return Mexico's Spanish sovereignty. Santa Anna's troops met and stopped a small invasion force at Tampico. The ringleaders were shot, and the government stripped all remaining Spaniards of bureaucratic office, banished Spanish officers from the military, and later expelled many other middle-class Spaniards. This caused economic disturbances, for it meant that people of ability and experience left the country, and took their capital along. Santa Anna and the conservatives compelled Guerrero to resign. Anastasio Bustamante, a general and a physician, held office for almost three years and discreetly followed in his policy the counsel of the conservative Lucas Alamán, a cabinet minister since Victoria's election. Alamán, who now became virtual dictator, wished to industrialize Mexico. As he did not want to expropriate the property of the clergy or divide up the great haciendas, either of which would have supplied the government with additional funds, he created an industrial loan bank, which had charge of buying machinery abroad and having it installed where it was best suited. It was, as we would say now, an institution for the promotion and planning of development. American and French technicians were called in to train Mexicans. Several textile mills were established in Puebla, and a paper mill was set up. These were the nuclei of two Mexican industries that are still prospering.

But this was not enough to ensure domestic tranquillity. Guerrero rebelled and was captured and executed by Bustamante's conservative government in 1831. This provoked a new coup by the liberals, led by that political chameleon Santa Anna, and that was followed by a civil war that lasted almost a year. Bustamante, who owed his present position as president to Santa Anna, now found himself attacked as a reactionary by the same general. Bustamante resigned under pressure and a provisional president was named for three months. Subsequently in January, 1833, Santa Anna was elected, with an enthusiastic liberal, Valentín Gómez Farías, as vice-president. The latter was to be the real head of government, for the general, with the approval of congress, retired to one of his haciendas. Elected by the liberals, Santa Anna had no stomach for the strong measures which his backers planned to bring against the privileges of the Church and the military, so he removed himself from any possible responsibility for their actions.

Gómez Farías' moves against the Church began when he demanded from the Vatican continuation of the system of "royal patronage" which had given the king of Spain the right to nominate bishops for appointment. This meant the annulment of several papal appointments of bishops, and naturally the clergy was incensed. They were still more deeply disturbed by the creation of a government office of Public Instruction, which favored establishment of lay teaching, thus depriving the clergy of their educational monopoly. The Jesuits were expelled, ecclesiastical tithing suspended, the Church-run University of Mexico closed. The California missions were secularized and their property was expropriated, and in return the missionaries received a salary from the government. Gómez Farías added the enmity of the army to that of clergy when he suppressed special ecclesiastical and military privileges by which priests and officers were tried by their peers and not by civil judges. Sixteen months after Gómez Farías had assumed office, there was an abortive pronunciamento. This and evidence of a religious resurgence brought on by a plague of cholera prompted Santa Anna to leave his hacienda and return to the presidency—this time not as a liberal, but as a conservative, for it looked to him as if the tide was turning against the liberals.

He promptly annulled Gómez Farías' reforms. Several liberal governors refused to recognize Santa Anna; but their forces were defeated. The general, lauded in the churches and in the salons, became a hero to the people, for the clergy, who were now supporting him, had great influence with the man in the street. Santa Anna, ambitious man that he was, wanted a stronger government, and in 1835, a conservative congress voted a new constitution of the centralist type, annulling the federal system. Santa Anna withdrew once again, this time leaving the reins of government in the hands of the new vice-president, General Miguel Barragán.

Much more important than these internal squabblings was the problem of Texas, which was first posed in Santa Anna's administration and was to dominate Mexican sentiment for many years. In 1821 the viceroy had given permission to Moses Austin, an American impresario and land agent, to settle three hundred families from the Louisiana Territory in the Mexican state of Texas, provided that they were Catholics and promised to obey the Spanish law. Moses Austin died before his dream was realized. But later that year, after Mexico had won its independence, Austin's son, Stephen, succeeded in having the new republic recognize this concession. Each homesteading family was guaranteed 640 acres or more at low cost and tax free for the first six years. Mexico, whose economic situation was grave, welcomed this opportunity to populate and exploit its vast, nearly uninhabited northern lands. Immigration proceeded rapidly; by 1830 some 25,000 English-speaking naturalized Mexican citizens were living in the territory. But the good faith which had characterized the original agreement was beginning to wane. The requirement that all settlers be Catholic was not being met, and the outsiders were beginning to show an independence of spirit that was worrisome to the Mexican government. There were early indications of the conflict that would develop: in 1826 one of the colonists, Haden Edwards, quarreled with some of the other titleholders and was expelled from the state. He countered by raising a small rebellion among his followers and proclaiming the Free Republic of Fredonia. When Austin's group supported the Mexican government instead of Edwards, the insurrection collapsed. Everything appeared to return to a state of peaceful coexistence, though tensions had now arisen and the United States government twice offered to purchase Texas, the first time at a price of one million dollars, the second at five million.

In 1835, there were in Texas perhaps twenty thousand Anglos, or English-speaking whites, and a thousand Negro slaves who cultivated cotton and sugar cane. Prohibited by the Missouri Compromise from opening up any new lands north of the 36° 30' parallel to slavery, the Americans had seen Texas as a desirable place to extend their agricultural system. But the Mexicans, who had outlawed slavery elsewhere in the country but had given grudging concessions to the Anglo-Americans, watched uneasily as the numbers grew.

To keep the foreign element from getting any stronger, President Bustamante and Secretary Alamán sponsored a law stemming further immigration, increasing the taxes, and restricting trade across the border, but there was no practical way to patrol and enforce the laws in the vast region. About the same time, the state of Texas was joined with that of Coahuila in an effort to tilt the population scales in favor of the Spanish-speaking Mexicans.

After the liberal triumph of the Gómez Farías faction in 1833, Austin and the other Texas Anglos petitioned unsuccessfully for independent statehood within the Mexican union. On the return trip to Texas he was arrested on charges of treason and imprisoned for eighteen months. Finally, the majority of the settlers, contrary to the terms of the original concession, were now not Catholics, but avowed Protestants, and held a contemptuous attitude toward the Church, which was so powerful in Mexico under the conservatives. To complicate matters, the Southern politicians in Washington were urging the addition of Texas to the Union, for they hoped by this means to make up for the loss of influence suffered at the hands of Northern abolitionists.

With Santa Anna's return and his rescinding of the federal constitution in 1835, the settlers had a pretext to proclaim the independence of Texas. In addition to Austin, once again active in Texas, encouragement was given by a fugitive Mexican, Lorenzo de Zavala, who had been a minister in the first Mexican republican government, and who now, seeing the conservatives in power, hoped to make Texas a bulwark and model of liberal government. The proclamation of independence had been provisional, until such time as the federal constitution should be re-established in Mexico. Zavala believed in this qualification, but the settlers had other plans.

The Texans, who had a political leader in the person of Stephen Austin, now found a military leader in the picturesque adventurer Sam Houston. Houston, who had been a congressman and governor of Tennessee, had some years earlier suffered a personal crisis and retreated from the white man's world to live as an adopted son of the Cherokees. There his intemperance had earned him the name "Big Drunk"; but in 1833 he took hold of himself and headed for Texas, determined to rebuild his political career and serve his old friend and leader, Andrew Jackson. Houston was soon in the thick of the Texan revolt and he sent several dispatches to the American president advising him that the territory was ripe for American intervention.

Meanwhile, the armed skirmishes between the Anglos and the Mexican troops deployed in Texas escalated into real warfare. Free lances like Davy Crockett and Jim Bowie joined the Anglos, and Santa Anna countered by leading a small army of some six thousand men into rebel country. Some idea of the catch-as-catch-can nature of the Mexican dictator's army can be derived from knowing that the greater part of

his troops were peons from haciendas or in the employ of the public
works contractors to whom he had given contracts and from whom, as
a *quid pro quo,* he had demanded this blood tax.

Santa Anna reached San Antonio in February, 1836, and found it
defended by a force of only 150, who had taken their stand behind the
stout fortification of the Alamo, a former Franciscan mission. Despite
desperate calls for aid, only thirty-odd Americans responded and
slipped into the doomed fortress. After a ten-day siege, Santa Anna's
troops surged over the walls and at their leader's direction rounded up
and put to death all the survivors. Then oil was poured over the heaped
up bodies and the lot set afire. This bloody event and the massacre
shortly after at the town of Goliad further enhanced the determination
of the Anglos to achieve independence, a decision which they had
formally declared at the height of the siege, but which they now began
to put into meaningful action. Houston was named commander in
chief of the rebel army.

Santa Anna's success at the Alamo made him a savior in the eyes of
the Mexican people. Not even the rout he suffered in late April at the
hands of Houston's troops shook their faith. That battle occurred early
on the morning of April 21 at the San Jacinto River, where Houston's
men caught them by surprise. With shouts of "Remember the Alamo,"
the ragtag Anglo troops captured Santa Anna and drove his army back.
The Mexican dictator bought his liberty by signing a secret treaty with
Houston to the effect that he would prepare the way for Mexico's
recognition of Texan independence. Then the two signed a public
armistice by which the Mexican armies would withdraw forever beyond the Rio Grande (or the Río Bravo, as it is called in Mexico).
Texas was now free in fact, if not in legal terms. The general, after
further talks with Jackson in Washington, was taken by sea to Veracruz and released. He immediately disclaimed his promises, saying,
"You have kept me too long. The presidency will have passed into
other hands; and on my return, I shall have to retire to my hacienda,
shorn of all power, and incapable, however desirous of carrying out
my pledges." Indeed, he was greeted by his countrymen with suspicion
and did withdraw from the center of the ring for a time. The independent republic of Texas was proclaimed in September, 1836, and the
advisability of annexing Texas as an American state was urgently de-

*Wounded but victorious, Sam Houston offers his hand to the defeated Santa
Anna after the battle of San Jacinto, April 21, 1836.*

bated in Washington. Americans had to weigh the threat of outright war with Mexico and the dislocation caused by bringing a slave state into the Union, against the chance to expand United States frontiers.

Meanwhile, the international difficulties of the still-young country were by no means over. Following the death of Ferdinand VII, Spain in 1836 recognized the independence of her former colony, and thus ended Mexico's fears of reconquest. But France was about to become a new headache.

In 1837, Bustamante, recently returned from European exile, once again succeeded to the presidency. He was obliged to suppress several federalist rebellions. He was also confronted with some seemingly insignificant negotiations with France. The French minister had lodged a claim on behalf of his government for 800,000 pesos in indemnities for the losses French nationals had undergone during the riots of 1828. Particularly indignant was a pastry shop owner, who had suffered humiliation and the loss of all his pastries at the hands of some riotous Mexican officers, and the subsequent Mexican-French troubles became known as the Pastry War.

In January, 1838, the French ambassador presented an ultimatum and, unsatisfied, returned to France. A small fleet of French vessels then blockaded Veracruz and six months of unproductive talks were begun. Then, in November, the fleet bombarded the fort of Veracruz, which surrendered. (Santa Anna, always skillful in profiting by popular sentiment, declared his opposition to the surrender.) The French landed, intending to seize Santa Anna, but he fled, reportedly in his underwear, whereupon the French retired. As they withdrew they were attacked by troops that the general had hastily regrouped; he lost a leg when he was struck with a cannon ball.

The French continued to press for a settlement. At last a peace was signed and Mexico paid the indemnity of 800,000 pesos. Not even war could interrupt the country's bitter political struggle; while Santa Anna had been cutting such a ridiculous figure at Veracruz, the federalist risings had continued in other parts of the country. Bustamante seemed too moderate to the conservatives. Once again they rallied around Santa Anna, and in 1841 staged a coup that unseated Bustamante and brought to power the general who had lost Texas.

Santa Anna's popularity now was enormous—the government had

bestowed upon him the title Benemerito de la Patria (Well-deserving of the Fatherland), and a huge and devoted throng attended ceremonies in which the general's severed leg was solemnly interred and a monument erected. His defeats appeared to endear him even more to the public. (To this day no historian has found a convincing explanation of this strange fascination. For Santa Anna was not extremely intelligent, nor was he a great orator, or a skillful general, or an efficient executive. All he had was a keen instinct for the advantageous moment and the ability to come up holding the power. Perhaps what the Mexicans admired in him was that he was more ready than his adversaries, or as it is expressed in Mexico, *los madrugaba*—"he beat them to it.")

Santa Anna had seized power by taking advantage of the discontent with the new taxes the government had decreed. But once he was in the Palacio Nacional, the first thing he did was raise them again. When a constituent congress was elected, the liberal-federalists won out. The constitution they drafted was not to the general's liking (for Santa Anna's friends wanted an authoritarian constitution), and he stirred up a series of rebellions against congress. Finally, this body was replaced by a Junta Nacional—a sort of consultative assembly—named by Santa Anna, who drafted several "organic bases" (meaning a constitution) that were extremely centralist and gave much influence to the Church. Santa Anna was now virtually a dictator, refusing to account even to the Junta Nacional for his administration, and he showed signs of delusions of grandeur. He had a statue of himself erected in the capital, ordered luxurious uniforms for the army, and declared himself marshal—but he could not quell a new series of uprisings. He was arrested and banished to Cuba.

Santa Anna's centralism had impelled Yucatán, which was undergoing an economic crisis, to declare itself independent until such time as the federal regime should be restored. After a couple of years of fighting, peace was made, and Yucatán rejoined Mexico in 1843 with the understanding that her men should not be conscripted for military service and that taxes collected from her should be spent within her borders.

This long account of coups, wars, countercoups, congresses, and presidents may give the impression that Mexico was leading a chaotic existence. But all these things really affected only a very small number of citizens—politicians, military men, and the bureaucrats—and most people took notice of what was going on only when taxes on drink and food were raised or when men were forcibly recruited to swell the ranks of a rebel chief or of the government forces resisting him. One result of this was that the battles were not very deadly affairs, for those who took part were "summer soldiers" without training and entirely without enthusiasm. Still, the accumulation of coups and battles did cause a considerable number of deaths and maimings. It should be said that *coups d'état* were usually made in the provinces, for the peons of some hacendado or other who was backing the coup formed the bulk of the rebel forces at the time. Things were very different when the enemy was not a rebel troop or a few government battalions, but American forces. Although the latter were also hastily recruited raw militia, they were equipped with much more up-to-date arms and were more efficient than the Mexican troops. This was demonstrated in the war between Mexico and the United States. The version of this struggle that is current in Mexico will be given here. Readers may compare it with what they learned in school and draw their own conclusions.

First we must determine why Mexico arrived at such a perilous state. When the United States was created, Mexico had been more prosperous, better organized, and more cultivated than its northern neighbor; but three fourths of a century later, Mexico was dramatically poorer, less well organized, and culturally less developed. To say that this was because Mexico had no political stability is merely to evade the question. What was the reason for Mexico's not having political stability? To attribute it to the Mexicans' lack of preparation or to hint that they were lazy (which is totally false) or to say it was because they were dominated by the Church (which is only half true) is inadequate. In this writer's opinion, the answer is to be found in the comparison of the social structures of the two nations. In the United States, except in the South, there were no feudal survivals, and even at the beginning of the nineteenth century the limits on suffrage were disappearing. In Mexico, on the other hand, the great agricultural landholdings of a relatively few men were the basis of society, and this entailed social tensions that could be relieved only in violent action. That action may have appeared narrowly political but, at bottom, it really reflected the unconscious discontent of the majority of Mexicans with the kind of society in which they lived.

The fact is that in 1845 Mexico was a country with a legally democratic state organization and a society almost feudal in practice. We have seen how shaky the political situation was, and from that we may judge the fears of Mexicans—at least that small part of them that was politically informed—when they learned that the congress of the United States had approved the annexation of Texas. Mexicans familiar with their history recalled that in the preceding century a minister of King Charles III of Spain, the count of Aranda, had predicted that the new United States would first encroach upon Florida (as did happen) and then try to gain a foothold in New Spain. The more liberal were also aware that in Texas, where there had been almost no slaves in the Spanish colonial period, slavery now existed, and had been extended farther to the west in the unorganized territories of Utah and New Mexico, as Americans settled. There was a risk that Mexico, despite its abolition of slavery, might be reinfected.

President James K. Polk of the United States proposed to Mexico the purchase of what are now the states of California and New Mexico. The Texans had asserted, and Santa Anna had ratified, that the southern boundary of their country was the Rio Grande, and the Polk administration adopted this claim. Mexico contended that the frontier was a little to the north of the river. Angered, the newly elected Mexican president, José Joaquín Herrera, recalled his Washington envoy and made visible efforts to mobilize the army. However, he privately sought means to conciliate without losing face, for the Mexican treasury was in ruins and the nation too underindustrialized to embark on any long-term military enterprises.

Public opinion forced him to reject an American envoy who had come to discuss a peaceful settlement; and shortly after, Herrera himself was rejected—unseated in a coup led by the fiery General Mariano Paredes. The new president was bent on revenge, and the United States responded by sending General Zachary Taylor and a body of four thousand men to take up defensive positions along the Rio Grande. Paredes met this show of force with a contingent of his own which was ordered to hold the Americans. Several weeks passed, however, while the Mexicans passively watched the American movements. Then, when

sufficient reinforcements had arrived, the Mexican general Mariano Arista engaged a small squadron of Americans, capturing them handily. Hostilities had now turned to open warfare.

This act of bravado was not followed by further Mexican triumphs. The Mexicans were repulsed at Palo Alto on the Texas side of the river and forced to withdraw south to Matamoros, where they were again defeated. In August, four months after his takeover, Paredes was pushed aside in favor of still another leader, the former vice-president Gómez Farías, who reinstated the liberal constitution of 1824 and made gestures toward strengthening the army. This upheaval provided Santa Anna with the opportunity he was waiting for. The old general had been exiled eighteen months earlier to Cuba, where he had spent his time watching cockfights and preparing for a comeback. He had approached President Polk with what now seems like a transparent scheme to regain power: he promised that if the Americans would grant his ship safe passage through their blockade of the Mexican coast, he would guarantee a prompt and friendly settlement of the boundary dispute, thus ending the war. Amazingly, Polk accepted the proposal and the double-dealing Santa Anna returned to take charge of the army, his guarantee forgotten.

Congress then named Santa Anna president and Gómez Farías vice-president. The public took new hope, for, in spite of all his earlier disasters, they still believed the general able to work miracles. And nothing less than a miracle was needed, since disillusionment with the governing system was so great that only seven states could be persuaded to furnish men and money for the war.

Santa Anna did what he could to firm up his political base and to quell a near civil war in Mexico City, and then at the end of September, 1846, he headed for San Luis Potosí to raise an army, just as Monterrey was falling to the Americans. During the remaining months of the year, he rounded up an army of several thousand men, and to obtain needed funds he ordered the expropriation and sale at auction of Church property. By late January he was ready to make the 200-mile march northwestward toward Saltillo, where he planned to engage Zachary Taylor's army. His men arrived at nearby Buena Vista exhausted, their numbers considerably reduced by defections, disease, and exposure to severe weather; and on February 22 and 23, in the

A nineteenth-century Indian market offers a sumptuous array of foods.

narrow pass known as La Angostura, they were routed, chiefly because of the great superiority of enemy artillery. The general retreated south to Mexico City only to learn that the undefended city of Veracruz had fallen after seven days' bombardment by an American naval squadron. The enemy was reported heading inland for Mexico City.

Santa Anna then made plans to thwart the invasion at the mountain pass of Cerro Gordo on the road to Mexico City, but the Americans outmaneuvered him again. In Jalapa, they rang up another victory, and still others at Contreras and Churubusco. A truce was declared on August 24 and negotiations were begun. Mexico was disposed to recognize the annexation of Texas, but Polk now demanded the cession of California, New Mexico, and part of northern Mexico, as well as the right of way through the Isthmus of Chapultepec, to give easier access to the west. The negotiations were unsuccessful, but they gave Santa Anna two weeks in which to regroup his forces. The truce over, the invaders resumed their march, and after several days' fighting approached the capital.

The Mexicans fought furiously for three weeks, on an isthmus between the two lakes of Texcoco (which are dried up now). In this fighting the military cadets of Chapultepec Castle won distinction—all were killed—some reportedly throwing themselves over the cliffs rather than be captured—and this was the origin of a kind of national cult for what Mexicans call "the Child Heroes." The lack of warlike spirit on the battlefield, and on the contrary the amount of martial spirit shown at the gates of the capital, which surprised the American soldiers, were owing to the differences in the army's composition: the forces on the battlefield were Indians from the haciendas, who in many cases did not consider themselves Mexicans at all but rather members of their own tribes, and who resented having been separated from them to fight; whereas those who fought at the gates of the capital were mestizos and whites, people of the middle class and students, who had definite ideas about their nation and their political credo. This spirit even infected Santa Anna, who for the first time in his life appeared to have some object besides personal profit. But this did not last long. The American forces finally took the capital, and Santa Anna fled. The only authority left was the congress. After some desperate attempts to continue the war in Puebla, discouragement seized the government.

The Mexican congress was inclined to negotiate, but at the same time as the war with the United States was being waged, the Yaqui Indians of the Pacific Coast and the Mayas in Yucatán had rebelled. The deputies deposed Santa Anna, and as no one wanted to be president, the head of the supreme court, in accordance with the constitution, had to assume the succession. He was Manuel de la Peña y Peña. He removed the government to Querétaro, where there were no United States troops, and ordered that Santa Anna be tried for incompetence. But the general asked the Americans for safe conduct, and went into exile in Jamaica.

Peña y Peña's negotiations with the United States resulted in the Treaty of Guadalupe Hidalgo signed just outside the capital on the second of February, 1848. By this treaty Mexico ceded to the United States what is now Utah, Nevada, and California, all New Mexico and Arizona north of the Gila River, and parts of Colorado and Wyoming, and recognized the annexation of Texas. The country lost 863,000 square miles, nearly half its former territory. For these losses the United States paid a compensatory sum of fifteen million dollars.

Not everyone in the United States had approved of the war. Lincoln and some other congressmen had condemned it as anticonstitutional, and Henry David Thoreau protested against what he regarded as an unjust war by refusing to pay his poll tax, for which he was briefly jailed. When Emerson went to visit him and asked, "Henry, what are you doing in there?" Thoreau retorted, "Waldo, what are you doing out there?" Lincoln, by the way, is more admired in Mexico for his stand concerning the war than for the abolition of slavery.

In the three years of off-and-on warfare, the Mexicans were always outmatched in artillery, supplies, and in leadership, but they are still proud today that in spite of these disadvantages they were able to offer resistance from all sides. The country emerged from the conflict humiliated, ruined, and demoralized—it was to be a decade before the new generation would dare to look into the future. For the moment, life was a matter of surviving the disaster.

Before this could be brought about, Mexico had once again to submit to the mercies of the incredible Santa Anna, with his special gift for turning public failures into personal successes. He did not reappear until the country's wretched treasury had been somewhat healed of its

OVERLEAF: *An 1868 painting by Luís Coto shows the railroad terminal of Guadalupe. The other end of the line was Mexico City, three miles away.*

wounds, thanks again to President José Joaquín Herrera, who had returned to office. Herrera had established the National Bank, consolidated part of the public debt, and began construction of Mexico's first railroad, even while he was confronted by army mutinies and numerous uprisings, the most important being another civil war in Yucatán, the so-called War of the Castas (people of color).

During the Mexican-American war, the state of Yucatán had declared itself neutral and it had armed an Indian army to maintain its position. Now that the war was over, these descendants of the Mayas rebelled, demanding protection of their lands. In 1847 they proceeded to harass the whites, with the backing of England, which was then in a dispute with the United States over dominion in Central America. Finally, in 1850, an accord with the rebels was reached. It abolished the personal tax paid by the Indians, forbade the practice of selling Indians into virtual slavery, and guaranteed them protection of their ejidos. Once peace was restored, the whites ignored in practice the promises they had made.

With Mexico's continuing instability, no leader could maintain his position for long and there were three successive provisional presidents, until finally Santa Anna was again elected in 1853. He set up a "perpetual dictatorship," which lasted until 1855. He persecuted journalists and intellectuals who objected to his highhanded rule, imprisoning and later deporting two future leaders of the reform movement: Benito Juárez of Oaxaca and Melchor Ocampo of Michoacán. The conservative opposition demanded that a monarchy be proclaimed with a European prince on the throne. They got half their wish: Santa Anna awarded himself the title "His Most Supreme Highness," and named a successor. But by now those who had been young at the time of the war with the United States, and were not under the spell of the Santa Anna myth and legend, began to participate in politics. Their indignation reached a high point when the United States sought to purchase the frontier territory known as the Mesilla (now the southern parts of Arizona and New Mexico) as a railway corridor to the Pacific. Instead of submitting the purchase bid to arbitration, as prescribed by the Treaty of Guadalupe Hidalgo, Santa Anna agreed to sell the 45,000 square miles for ten million dollars. (The army's loyalty was directly related to Santa Anna's ability to meet the payroll, and his extravagance had brought the exchequer dangerously low.) The transaction was known as the Gadsden Purchase, after James Gadsden, who negotiated it for the United States.

The new generation, most of them liberals, looked around for a leader, and found their man in the Indian general Juan Álvarez, a former insurgent of the Independence period. He led an uprising in Ayutla, in the state of Guerrero, and there in March, 1854, announced the liberals' plan for the re-establishment of democracy and the fortifying of federalism by means of a new constitution; the plan also promised to effect the separation of Church and State and to expropriate the property of the clergy. The uprising immediately took the dimensions of a popular movement. Guerrillas arose in every corner of the country. In August, 1855, after his forces had met repeated defeats, Santa Anna took ship at Veracruz and fled to South America. He was to live another twenty years, making several attempts to return to Mexico, each of which was met with deportation. He was allowed to come home in 1874 and he died, all but penniless, in Mexico City two years later.

The liberals had triumphed; in October, 1855, Álvarez was elected president pro tem. But disputes immediately arose in the heart of the government between the *puros,* who advocated immediate adoption of the promised measures, and the *moderados,* who wanted to smooth them down and get them adopted. Most controversial was the law pushed through by Álvarez' minister of justice, Benito Juárez, who took direct aim at ecclesiastical and military privilege when he denied all special courts jurisdiction in civil matters. Unequipped by training or temperament to hold the disputing factions together, Álvarez resigned in December—only two months after assuming office—naming as his provisional successor General Ignacio Comonfort, a moderate who had been at his side in the uprising and had since served in his cabinet as minister of war.

Under Comonfort, the program to diminish the Church continued. The Jesuits were suppressed, and then in June, 1856, the drastic Ley Lerdo (a law named for its chief drafter, Miguel Lerdo de Tejada) was passed. The Lerdo law ordered that the Church divest itself of all lands not specifically devoted to religious functions (that is, lands upon which no churches or ecclesiastical buildings stood) and that these lands be sold to existing tenants. By this means, it was hoped, the vast

Church-owned agricultural holdings would be made available for purchase at reasonable cost to the landless lower classes, thus creating almost overnight a nation of small landowners, presumably a more stable popular base for the democracy which the liberals hoped to create. But in practice, the mass sell-off benefited few if any peasants, for they had not the cash for such purchases; instead, it was foreign investors and the Creole middle class who were the greatest beneficiaries of this policy, becoming Mexico's new landed aristocracy. The Church, though it no longer was Mexico's chief landowner, now received large sums of money with which to enforce its political power. And the State, which had anticipated a considerable inflow of tax money resulting from a tax on the sale of the real estate, gathered a great deal less than expected.

Meanwhile, the constituent congress, having met again, offered a new constitution early in 1857. Like the Ley Lerdo, it was filled with radical curtailments of Church power, including the establishment of secular education, civil rights for priests and nuns, freedom of speech and press, freedom of assembly, prohibition of Church courts, and State rather than Church control over the right to worship freely. Despite the fact that the pope in Rome threatened to excommunicate any Catholic who ratified the new constitution, the majority of congressmen and deputies signed it into law.

As might have been expected, the new constitution displeased both the more radical liberals and conservatives, but its authors, chiefly "pure" liberals, were optimistic. However, they had not counted on the wavering resolve of their chosen leader Comonfort who, despite his declarations against the Church, shrank from carrying out some of the programs his government outlined. And he was dissatisfied with the superior powers which the legislative branch had over the executive. While he was still considering what action he might take, the Church found a new hero: General Félix Zuloaga, who staged a coup in Tacubaya, at the very gates of Mexico City. Zuloaga rejected the new constitution and demanded that Comonfort convoke a new constituent congress, one more sympathetic to the Church. But the president was no more able to cope with the conservatives than with the liberals; resigning, he fled the country, leaving Zuloaga in charge. However, for the first time in the country's history, matters did not end

The Austrian archduke Maximilian and his royal Belgian wife, Carlota, in a portrait painted before their ill-fated departure for Mexico

with the deposition of the president. According to the constitution which Zuloaga had set aside, the president of the supreme court was vice-president of the nation. And under Comonfort the president of the supreme court was that exceptional personage Benito Juárez. A pure-blooded Zapotec Indian, and a lawyer, he had been governor of his native state of Oaxaca. Then after several months' exile in the United States, he returned to join Álvarez and was thereafter elected vice-president, the second most powerful man in the nation, in 1857. To everyone's surprise, Juárez, without an army to back him, without any more force than that of law, declared that constitutionally he was president. A new, bloody civil war broke out, one that would last three years.

During the War of the Reform, as it came to be known, there were two governments: the conservative-centralist, in Mexico City, and the liberal-federalist government headed by Juárez, which was forced to wander from city to city. Juárez continued to lose ground and the conservative forces soon were in command of the central plateau. The liberal government was driven to the Pacific Coast, took ship for Panama, crossed to the east coast, and sailed up to Veracruz. Learning from his defeats, Juárez set about the formation of a liberal army.

The liberals, in their eagerness to win recognition from the United States, had signed an accord, known as the McLane-Ocampo Treaty, by which Mexico conceded to the United States the perpetual right of way over the Isthmus of Tehuantepec and the right to intervene if any situation became grave enough to endanger the lives of Americans. Included was an agreement to make the United States the most favored nation in tariff measures. Luckily for Mexico, the United States senate never ratified the treaty.

Washington nevertheless recognized Juárez' government and granted his petition that the United States send ships to Veracruz to cut off a fleet that was preparing a naval assault on the city. In 1860 the liberal forces, now experienced fighters, began to win battles, at the same time as the conservatives were being torn by disagreement and by coups in which one leader after another was elevated to the presidency. This made it possible for the liberals, on New Year's Day, 1861, to enter Mexico City and put an end to the civil war.

In the next to last year of the war, Juárez, then in Veracruz, had

promulgated a group of measures, called Reform Laws, in anticipation
of victory. This time Church property was to be nationalized outright
rather than auctioned off to the profit of Church coffers. The expropriated holdings were to be used as collateral for the credits the United
States had extended to Juárez. Other laws secularized education and
the cemeteries, created a civil register, and established freedom of
worship. Juárez had also recalled the envoy to the Vatican, and expelled a number of leading clergymen including the archbishop of
Mexico.

These laws had far-reaching consequences. By not touching the great
private landholdings, but only those held by the Church, the laws made
it possible for the latifundists, or owners of the large landholdings,
to acquire the Church lands at auction. Although some elements of the
middle class bought houses and land, the laws were generally bene-
ficial to the latifundists. The Church excommunicated all those who
bought the expropriated lands and buildings, but this deterred few
people, who fully expected to find a way to lift the sentence eventually.
And that was the way it happened some years later, when the Church
offered to forgive in return for alms.

Another consequence of the Reform Laws was the virtual disappear-
ance of the ejidos. The liberals believed that all property should be
individually owned; as a result they divided up the ejidos and gave
each individual member of a commune a piece of land. But the peasants
had never owned any land individually, and, besides, they were very
poor. It was not long before the peasants sold their lands to city people
or neighboring latifundists, or before the latter, making use of trickery
or force, despoiled them of their property. In this way, contrary to the
liberals' intentions, the Reform Laws strengthened the latifundiary
system.

Juárez also had to cope with huge claims lodged by France, Spain,
and England on behalf of their own nationals. Chief among them was
a debt contracted by the conservative government with the Swiss
banker Jean-Baptiste Jecker. In exchange for a promised loan of 15
million dollars (only 10 per cent of which was actually delivered),
Jecker was to receive, in amortization and interest payments, 16.8 million dollars. When Juárez declared a two-year moratorium on all ex-
ternal national debts, Jecker, who became a French citizen, brought

influence to bear on his adopted government to demand immediate repayment by the liberals; and this served as a trampoline for conservative acrobatics.

The conservatives had not given up the idea of regaining power. The exiled General Juan Almonte, a natural son of the insurgent Morelos, who perhaps because he was angry about his origins fought with the conservatives, entered into negotiations in Paris with the government of Napoleon III. In exchange for foreign support in his bid for the presidency, Almonte promised to guarantee their economic claim. He succeeded in getting France to form an alliance with Spain and England to send an expedition to collect Mexico's foreign debt. The United States was in the midst of its Civil War, and this prevented Washington from enforcing the Monroe Doctrine (which forbade all foreign interference in the affairs of the Western Hemisphere). British, French, and Spanish warships made for Veracruz.

Juárez' representative negotiated with the European triple alliance and thought he had persuaded the three envoys to accept a peaceful solution in the light of Mexico's dire economic straits. But in reality Napoleon III had much larger goals in mind than securing Jecker's dubious claim, and he was only waiting for the right moment to press still more impossible claims so that he would have an excuse to send in his troops and eventually to install a monarch of his choosing. The representatives of London and Madrid, realizing now that they were being played as pawns in France's imperialist scheme and having no desire to plunge into a profitless war, broke off the alliance and reembarked their forces on April 28, 1862.

While these events were taking shape, the French helped Almonte and some of his exiled followers slip back into their country and reorganize the conservative forces. Then with a force of three thousand men the French interventionists marched toward Mexico City, claiming that nothing less than armed might would avenge the many insults suffered by them. To everyone's surprise, the tattered Mexican resistance was able to repel the first attack on Puebla fought on May 5 (since celebrated as a day glorious in Mexican history). Shocked and angered by this humiliation, Napoleon dispatched another 28,000 reinforcements, putting General Élie Forey in charge. The enlarged attack proved too much for Juárez' government, and realizing that there was

no way the liberals could resist successfully, the president ordered his administration to evacuate Mexico City. Just a little more than two years after it had concluded the war with the conservatives, Juárez' government resumed its peripatetic career. It was to last another five years.

Meantime, the Mexican conservatives had sent a delegation to Europe to seek out a king. The man who posed the fewest problems to the chancelleries was the Austrian archduke Maximilian (brother of the Austrian emperor, Franz Josef), an intelligent but indecisive young man, then about thirty, who was married to the Belgian princess Carlota, an ambitious woman. Maximilian made his acceptance conditional upon the Mexican people's approval of his accession to the throne, and the conservatives organized a plebiscite that, naturally, was favorable to him. He also signed a treaty with Napoleon III in which France promised to keep supportive troops in Mexico until 1867, in exchange for which the new emperor pledged to pay all the French expenses of intervention, past and future, plus all the claims lodged by Spain, England, and France in 1861. Maximilian also undertook

The emperor Maximilian and two of his generals before a firing squad. The execution took place on June 19, 1867, in Querétaro.

a loan from French bankers to tide him over until Mexico's financial affairs had been set in order. (What with a huge discount rate and interest deducted on the earlier Mexican debt, only a third of this sum was available for spending.) In June, 1864, Maximilian was crowned in Mexico City. In the process, he had just multiplied the impoverished nation's national debt by three.

It was not long before the conservatives were disappointed in him, for he turned out to be a moderate liberal who wanted to protect the Indians, promote social legislation, and even encourage a measure of freedom of thought. The Church, which had supported him, now withdrew its backing. There was friction between the Mexican conservative generals and the French generals, who took their orders from Napoleon III while drawing their pay from the ever-diminishing Mexican exchequer. Everyone was being blamed for the financial state of the nation and so the French took charge of the money too. Indeed, Maximilian was no man to save a moribund economy. He was slow to realize that the tales of El Dorado which he had been plied with while in Europe were wholly false. And both he and his empress, Carlota, had a taste for pomp and luxury; dissatisfied with the vast and drafty National Palace, they moved to the smaller summer castle in Chapultepec Park, which they set about remodeling. And a great four-mile-long walk (which today, paradoxically, is called Paseo de la Reforma and is one of the most beautiful and spacious boulevards in the world) was laid out between the royal residence and the geographical center of the city. But while the *mariachis* (street musicians, whose name is a corruption of the French word *mariage,* because they traditionally performed at weddings) were lauding the empress, the war was continuing in many parts of the country. Guerrilla bands arose, and Juárez reorganized the republican army. His black carriage continued to go from village to village and from city to city depending on the fortunes of war.

After Prussia defeated the Austrian forces at the Battle of Sadowa and when the Civil War in the United States ended, the situation began to be altered. Napoleon III was eager to repatriate his soldiers, Lincoln recognized the Juárez government; Secretary of State William Henry Seward reminded the court at Paris of the Monroe Doctrine and demanded the withdrawal of French forces from Mexico. In the spring of 1866, Napoleon announced to Maximilian that he intended to call his soldiers home. By March of the following year there were no more French forces in Mexico.

That being the case, the republican army was able to advance from the north, equipped now with armaments bought in the United States. Maximilian had only Mexican soldiers, with scant enthusiasm for his cause, although his generals, trained in the earlier civil war, were ambitious and energetic. He wanted to abdicate, but Carlota persuaded him to wait while she went to Europe, seeking aid first from Napoleon III, then from the pope, all to no avail. While at the Vatican, she suffered a nervous breakdown, precipitated perhaps by the rebuffs she had encountered. (She was to live on for many years until 1927, shut away in a castle near Brussels.)

Again Maximilian expressed his wish to abdicate, but the conservative generals persuaded him that they would be able to win. They maneuvered to bring about a decisive battle, and concentrated their forces, which numbered barely 9,000, at Querétaro, where they were faced by 21,000 republicans. On May 15, 1867, the city fell to Juárez' troops. Maximilian and two of his generals were captured, tried, and a month later executed. The empire, and the conservatives who had brought it to Mexico, were ousted, and from that time on the liberals held the government.

While the battles had been in progress in the mountains and around the cities, in those parts of the country that enjoyed a transitory peace, factories had been built and a large number of the artisans had become industrial workers; some had become businessmen. But the country remained essentially agricultural and latifundist.

Political questions—the role of the Church, the choice of monarchy or republic, of centralism or federalism—had been settled by Juárez' victories in the two civil wars while his government had been moving from pillar to post. Mexico was a definitely federal, lay, republican, and liberal state. Her long and painful apprenticeship had ended. And now she would begin to mature.

CHAPTER V

FROM
JUÁREZ TO DÍAZ

The country was exhausted and weary after two wars with foreign powers and so many civil conflicts. Although the armies involved had been small and the battles relatively limited, the total of casualties was considerable. Mexico wanted peace.

This was no vague yearning. During the half century of struggle a series of economic elements, for whose development peace was essential, had come to the fore. Although it may seem strange, industry had been prospering, and this had led to the formation of a new bourgeois or entrepreneurial class, as yet small, and of a working class that was beginning to be organized, and among whose members the works of Spanish anarchists and of Mikhail Bakunin, and to a lesser extent the works of Karl Marx, were circulating. Agriculture had been somewhat modernized, many once-abandoned lands had been cultivated, and the country was exporting not only minerals but other raw materials.

With more modern arms available, future civil wars would produce still more devastation, and it would be impossible to contain and isolate them. Hence, the industrialists and hacendados were fearful of any new disturbances. Furthermore, although in earlier days the ha-

Muralist José Clemente Orozco paints the face of Benito Juárez against a background of fire symbolizing the struggles of the reform movement.

cendados themselves had intervened in politics, arming their peons to fight, some for the liberal side, some for the conservative, they now wanted to stay out of the never-ending struggles for power, to preserve the new working force which was beginning to gain special skills and therefore was not easily replaced. A civil war would leave factories and plantations without experienced workers.

Despite the mass expulsion of the Spaniards in the earlier years of independence, after the country's autonomy was recognized by Spain there came an immigration of Spaniards, to whom were added Frenchmen, Swiss, Germans, and Americans. These immigrants usually devoted themselves to industry and trade, and when they had accumulated some savings invested their money in land. Thus, while the Mexicans had been giving all their attention to their internal struggles, the immigrants had been consolidating personal gains. The chance to acquire property either at the expense of the Church or the Indians' ejidos, and to exploit cheap labor, was a factor of which these immigrants did not fail to take advantage.

After Maximilian's empire fell, another generation of Frenchmen remained in the country and became participants in its economic life. It is odd that, although there was ill feeling toward Spain because she had been the mother country—an antagonism kept alive by the liberals, and never a personal or individual matter—there was no resentment toward the French or Americans. Possibly the French were accepted because of the attitude of Napoleon III's opponents at home. Critical of the imperial expedition, they had made a special effort to brand it as a private adventure of the emperor and not one that was supported by the nation as a whole. From his exile on the isle of Guernsey, Victor Hugo wrote a letter to Juárez in which, taking his metaphor from the grandiose topography of Mexico, he applauded the Mexican president for fighting "with mountainous blows." The reputations of Lincoln, Thoreau, and others saved the Americans from the wrath that would have naturally followed United States seizure of Texas. It was only later, as we shall see, that Mexico felt a wave of anti-Americanism—or antigringoism, as the Mexicans call it. (They had dubbed the North Americans *gringos* because, it is said, United States troops, during the 1846–48 war, sang a marching song containing the phrase "green grow the rushes."

The Mexicans of the Santa Anna–Juárez period had been too deeply involved in being antiliberal or anticonservative to have time to be anti anything else. The conservatives had wanted the regime that followed the winning of independence to be a continuation of the Spanish colony, but without a viceroy; the liberals had wanted to wipe out all traces of colonialism and make a direct tie with the pre-Cortés era. In a sense, the Mexican people confirmed their independence with the definite victory of the liberals, since the conservatives had repeatedly called upon foreign powers to bolster their own regimes.

These internal struggles were an intellectual challenge and a stimulus. No matter how desperate the country's situation appeared to be—divided and bloodstained as it was—many people had faith in its future and tried to put Mexico in tune with the rest of the Western world, especially on the cultural plane. The poetry and drama of the period were simply imitations of those produced in Europe, but the novels, although none attained really high quality, revealed a desire to look squarely at the realities of Mexico. Although no name in Mexican culture of the first fifty years of independence is outstanding, there are many that could properly be put into the second or third class of any other country's list. The same may be said of the journalists, painters, and men of science.

Historiography was the field in which the Mexicans were outstanding. It was cultivated by the best minds of the country, as if they wanted to compensate in literature for the people's lack of sense of historical continuity. It was logical that this lack should have existed. In 1860 the majority of the Mexican population was mestizo; and the mestizo rejected, naturally enough, the idea that he was heir to a colonizing white father and a native mother who had been violated or seduced. This lack of roots in the past doubtless contributed to the increasing unrest, but, at the same time, it compelled Mexicans to look constantly toward the future, since they did not flatter themselves about their past.

For more than thirty years, after Maximilian's execution, Mexico proved to be a place of relative order and freedom from war. But in 1867 few would have read the future so brightly, for discord immediately arose among Juárez' victorious liberals when he returned with his government to the capital.

Juárez' presidential mandate had expired during the war with Maxi-

milian. In view of the impossibility of holding elections, the government prorogued the mandate until such time as the conflict be ended. One of its first steps when Juárez re-entered the capital in 1867 was to call elections. He was chosen over the opposing candidate, Porfirio Díaz, who had twice escaped from the French and fought against them during the entire war. The liberal party, then, had become divided. Since there were no organized conservatives, the moderate liberals came to occupy their place in the political spectrum. And when Juárez reduced the size of the army by two thirds, to lessen the risk of military coups and to decrease the drain on the economy, and sent some sixty thousand men home with no pensions and barely a thank you, great numbers of soldiers and officers automatically became Díaz supporters. For a time these tensions were suppressed and during this breathing spell more reform legislation was passed: a civil code of modern cast was promulgated, the law of *amparo* (a sort of habeas corpus) was developed; and efforts made to widen educational opportunities.

A commission headed by Gabino Barreda, a disciple of the French philosopher Auguste Comte and the positivist movement, was set up to explore an educational system. A law was later passed making it lay-controlled, free, and compulsory—at least on paper, as there were

A nineteenth-century painting provides an idealized view of woman laborers in a coal mine. In actuality, mining conditions were often brutal.

scant funds and few teachers to meet the demand. Outside the cities town councils and hacienda owners were directed to build primary schools, with limited results. Seven years later Mexico had 8,000 schools with 350,000 pupils attending, about one sixth of the school-age population. Barreda's positivist educational system, which would produce the next generation of political activists, was committed to replacing Mexico's traditionally spiritual orientation with a practical, scientific, antimetaphysical basis for education and thought. In this it was to provide ringing justification for the highly pragmatic, anti-civil-libertarian dictatorship that would succeed Juárez, but at the time of its inception it seemed only anticlerical.

A beginning was made on construction of a railway from Mexico City to Puebla and work resumed on a line to Veracruz, begun in 1850 but abandoned during the war. Tracks were also laid across the Isthmus of Tehuantepec—of significance to the United States, which, in the years before the building of the Panama Canal, welcomed an alternate route for linking up its own Atlantic and Pacific coasts.

In 1871 Juárez' term of office expired and a new election followed. Opposing Juárez were his long-time friend and vice-president Sebastián Lerdo de Tejada (brother of Miguel, who had written the laws directing the nationalization of clerical lands) and again, General Díaz. Juárez was the winner, but without obtaining the clear majority. Therefore, in accordance with the constitution, the chamber of deputies had to designate the president and Juárez was returned to office. But he aroused discontent in the army and there were several coups, all crushed. Díaz' followers alleged that the elections were rigged and called for a new organic law that would prohibit a president from succeeding himself, rescind some taxes, limit the powers of congress, and restore municipal autonomy. The struggle was still in progress when Juárez suffered a heart attack and died in 1872. Vice-President Lerdo, a Simon-pure liberal but an arrogant man, thus succeeded to the presidency. In the next election Lerdo won and Díaz was again the loser. In the midst of new revolts by the losing party, Lerdo accomplished the establishment of a senate to moderate the actions of the chamber, and had reform laws incorporated into the constitution— the same document that had been approved in 1857. In Lerdo's regime the railroad line from the capital to Veracruz was inaugurated, but he refused offers from American railroad builders to extend their lines into the northern part of Mexico, preferring to keep the country in its wild state, for, as he argued, "between the strong and the weak, [the] best [thing] is a desert."

In July, 1876, when his term expired, Lerdo again stood for election. But his domineering character had alienated even his own party and his claims to have won the election were not widely accepted. Díaz again headed a revolt. The rebels numbered 12,000 men, to the government's small force of 4,000. Díaz prevailed and Lerdo left for New York, after obtaining the Mexican congress' permission to leave the country without resigning. New elections gave the victory to Díaz, and now he was president, after having lost three times and led several revolts. In accord with a promise he had made during one of those uprisings, he persuaded congress to reform the constitution, making illegal the re-election of the president and of the state governors. But Díaz was thinking of his own future, and proposed only that the prohibition against second terms should be applied to men seeking two *successive* terms only.

Díaz' method of opposing various coups against him was to order that the rebels should be "shot at once." When his term ended in November, 1880, his popularity had disappeared. But the no re-election clause suited his purpose well. He managed the election of a friend, also a general, and continued to govern de facto through him as the power behind the throne. In 1884 came a new election and another triumph for Díaz, who again took up residence in the castle of Chapultepec, in which Maximilian and Carlota had lived. In 1887 he brought about a new constitutional reform, permitting his re-election, and the next year was again elected. In 1890 congress annulled the article forbidding re-election, and from then on Díaz was regularly returned to office until 1910. After 1892 almost no coups against Díaz were attempted, for the general had done away with militarism in the same way he had ended banditry—he had appointed the generals to posts as governors, ministers, or ambassadors, lavishing on them titles and privileges to win their allegiance just as he had enrolled the bandits in the rural police.

It should be remembered that Díaz came out of the Liberal Party and that this party supported his candidacy. But under him the label also applied to conservatives of the new liberal order. As he opened the country to foreign investment, many public works were undertaken —major harbors were deepened and rebuilt, water supply, canal, and drainage systems extended, roads and railway lines laid, telephone and telegraph communications linked up, and many factories and businesses established. For the first time American rather than European capital was favored, and mining concessions widely distributed. (Previously, Mexico had held legal title to all subsoil rights in the nation, continuing the old Spanish colonial policy which declared all underground riches the property of the Crown. Foreign investment in mining enterprises had thus been minimal until the new Díaz policy was put into effect.) In consequence Mexico's immediate budgetary problems were lessening and after years of foreign contempt she was passing into a time of international prestige. She would, however, pay dearly for her openhandedness to foreign investors in later years.

Díaz' efforts at modernizing Mexico also meant that the working classes were growing, and so was the owner group, and this brought the rise of new political movements. One, to the left, was formed by the trade unions and anarchist-syndicalist groups. Still numerically weak, but being constantly stimulated by the arrival of European immigrants, it put up a very active propaganda front. On the right, there was the movement of the new capitalists, a generation of men who had been educated under the positivist philosophy of Mexico's new school system and who considered order the fundamental element of progress. In the opinion of Barreda, the first positivist minister of education, the state was the guardian of the material order, in which the rights of each individual were limited by the rights of others. Wealth in the paternalistic view of the positivists was "a public force that society has placed in the hands of the rich for the common good and for progress." So long as the rich used their wealth to stimulate more material wealth in the national economy, they need justify their actions to no one. Or as the Sociedad Metodofila, a positivist organization, proclaimed, Mexico most needed the "self-sacrifice of superiors for inferiors; respect and veneration by inferiors toward superiors."

This position was finally expressed in political terms with the formation in 1892 of the Union Liberal Party, a party whose policies were framed by the positivists and led by an elite inner circle which came to be known somewhat mockingly as the *cientificos* because they affirmed that politics should be a science. With Díaz as the instrument of this policy they gave their own class greater commercial and economic freedom to make money. Still, their efforts at modernization did not include any attack on the agrarian latifundist structure of the nation, whose beneficiaries were Díaz' close friends and the social force on which he leaned for support. This they saw as a phase to be reached later; but before the masses could be readied Mexico must achieve nationhood.

Opposing the cientificos philosophically there was another factor of the upper bureaucracy, the so-called Reyistas, named after their leader General Bernardo Reyes, the excellent governor of Nuevo León, who aspired to succeed Díaz some day. The Reyistas, whose strength was principally in the northern border states, wanted Mexico to progress so that it might be able to achieve a modern army; they considered the Mexican people capable of informed citizenship. Díaz' policy, for thirty years, consisted of setting these two groups against each other, arbitrating between them, and using both of them. This he did with a great deal of sagacity, although he gave more and more weight to the ideas of the cientificos. The latter were to discover that there was a basic contradiction in their desire to make Mexico into an industrial country without altering its agrarian structure.

When her independence began, Mexico had six million inhabitants, and 20,000 farms. At the end of the nineteenth century there were thirteen million people but no comparable increase in farm ownership —only 17,000 more farms had been established. Ownership of land, instead of being extended to the broader base of the population— especially the Indians—had become further concentrated among the rich mestizos and Creoles and the foreigners. From colonial times on, the laws had fixed a maximum—albeit very high—limit to the number of acres anyone could hold. But in 1894 Díaz abolished even that ceiling; thereafter anyone with the funds and the favored treatment of the government could acquire as much land as he wished. Furthermore, Díaz established a land registry and ordained that anyone not able to show title to his land had to forfeit his holdings. The hacienda owners immediately rushed to grab up what was left of the ancient ejidos, as the Indians could rarely show anything like a formal title, tradition

A youthful General Porfirio Díaz is shown triumphantly entering Puebla.

having been sufficient proof before. And the new law also removed the old obligation to cultivate and populate land held. Díaz was so much in favor of distributing great properties, as a means of buying off his enemies and making friends for himself, that in the nine years from 1881 to 1889 another 14 per cent of the area of the country passed into the hands of influential families or individuals. In Baja California, for example, four men came to own nearly 30 million acres, something like a fifth of the republic's land. On the eve of the revolution, 3,000 families owned half the country; of the 10 million persons on the land, 9.5 million owned none of it. So many foreigners had been allowed to enter in the nineteenth century that 70 per cent of the cultivated land was now owned by Spaniards, many of whom did not choose even to live in Mexico. Another 15 per cent belonged to French, American, English, and other foreigners. Old colonial families—mestizos and Creoles who predated independence—held a mere 11 per cent.

This concentration of land in the hands of a relatively few wealthy men perpetuated a feudal colonial social structure. The adjective "feudal" is no exaggeration. There were haciendas within which were cities, dozens of villages, and large numbers of inhabitants, and the hacendado was a true feudal lord, to whom all the local authorities—alcaldes (mayors), judges, priests, and the police—were virtually subject. Although they supported Díaz, the hacendados maintained all-embracing power on their properties. And they were permitted, besides, to do as they pleased with the Indians in their territory—taking away the Indians' lands, pastures, woods, and waters.

Industry was becoming foreign-dominated to the same extent through the constant furnishing of capital from abroad. By the time the Díaz regime ended, investments in mining and industry were distributed thus: United States interests, 499 million pesos; British, 87 million; French, 10 million. Wealthy Mexicans, who had never been won over to industrialization, had only 29 million pesos invested in the modernization of their country. The social effects of modernization can be seen in the growth of certain skilled worker groups: in 1823, two years after independence, there were 44,800 miners and 2,800 textile workers; in 1854 the latter had increased to 12,000, in 1873 to 32,000 (of a total 43,000 industrial workers), and in 1880 the entire factory force had risen markedly to 80,000. Meanwhile, the number

of miners had risen to 70,000. In Díaz' time workers had an average
working day of 12.5 hours, seven days per week; in short, they had no
protection. Women and children were subject to the same conditions
as men.

But with an immense majority of the population living off the land
and buying few if any manufactured products, Mexican industry could
not keep pace with the growth rate elsewhere. Though agricultural
and raw material exports grew, manufactured goods remained limited
to a small urban market. The railroads afford an example of what this
fundamental contradiction meant. In the United States, the railroad
opened new lands for settlement, and those lands, in accordance with
the Homestead Act and other laws, were acquired by farmers. In
Mexico the railroads did not fulfill this role, which we might call one
of agrarian reform, since they crossed huge haciendas whose land was
not to be shared; there the railroads were confined to joining cities and
to facilitating the sale of the products of the haciendas, thus favoring
latifundism. The railroads in Mexico transported only the products of
the cities and the haciendas, while in the United States they transported
the products of thousands and hundreds of thousands of independent
farmers. What in the northern neighbor country was a factor of social
mobility, in the southern one was a factor in reinforcing social immo-
bility in the rural areas. Furthermore, these Mexican railways were
built with British capital, which subsequently was also used to develop
Mexico's oil resources in the northeast.

Many Spanish immigrants, and for that matter Europeans in general, brought new social ideas with them from the Old World. In this
way socialist and especially anarchist groups arose, and newspapers
appeared, printed at great effort and bearing dramatic titles: *El Hijo
del Trabajo* (The Son of Toil), *La Huelga* (The Strike), *La Communa*
(The Commune). Mutual aid societies were formed, and these constituted the only protection the workers had in case of illness, accident,
dismissal, and death. Attempts were also made to create phalansteries,
in line with the ideas of the French socialist Charles Fourier; and some
private schools for the children of workers were established. All these
early efforts were to produce a generation of organizers, the ones who
formed the first trade unions and merged about 1870 in the Gran
Círculo de Obreros (Great Council of Workers). Only when these

syndicates began to acquire some power and to call strikes (and win them) did some Catholic unions come into being, through the inspiration of priests; they had, however, only small success.

When the landholders needed labor they appealed to the government. A Díaz appointee, Governor Ramón Corral of Sonora state, for example, on various occasions ordered the army to round up forcibly the indigenous Yaqui Indians and transplant them from the Pacific Coast to the torrid Gulf Coast lands of Yucatán, where the cultivation of henequen (sisal hemp) was beginning, and to the Valle Nacional of Oaxaca, where tobacco was being raised. The Mayas, who had barely managed to survive the colonial age, were now similarly oppressed and decimated. But this method of enslavement could not be applied to mobilizing the semiskilled labor for the factories. Hence a certain amount of labor organization had to be tolerated.

Education of the peasant masses, which had been proclaimed a national goal under Juárez, still did not exist; there were no rural schools to furnish it. On the other hand, urban workers, in addition to their union schools, had available to them the public ones, insufficient in number, true, but generally staffed by teachers of liberal spirit. The sons of the middle class, which was growing so under Díaz' regime, were educated in private institutions, some religious and some secular, and attended the university.

The liberals, as has been noted, had for a long time the only existing formal party. It was very loosely structured, formed by personalities, without any real organization. With the advancing entrenchment of Díaz' government, which Mexicans were now beginning to regard as a dictatorship buttressed by elections, the Liberal Party was beginning to disintegrate, and political life was becoming limited to struggles for influence among the two factions of the upper bureaucracy that we have mentioned.

However, after 1900, it was possible to perceive a degree of disquiet in other, formerly unorganized, sectors of society: old-time liberals, union workers, and young men influenced by European ideas and rankled by the dogmatic positivism of the governing elite; peasants enraged by despoliation of their lands and water in the interests of the big landowners; professional men irritated by the growing influence of the Church in public life and education—all were elements that

In a rare moment of gentlemanly grace, Manuel Ocaranza, one of Mexico's hard-riding guerrilla fighters, poses for a formal portrait in 1866.

became more and more opposed to the regime. Satirical publications and others of a socialistic tendency appeared—but were often suspended, with their directors frequently winding up in jail. After 1900, there were spontaneous peasant rebellions, brutally put down, and long strikes which brought the strikers face to face with the troops.

Juárez had been a simple, determined man, who lived and died poor, who had always maintained the domination of civil power over the military, who had coursed all over the country in his black carriage and had kept contact with the people—at least with the middle classes. Díaz, on the contrary, was a soldier who solved problems not by means of negotiation, but with orders and often by forcible suppression. He liked pomp and uniforms, and as he grew older he became more fond of flattery and grandiose exhibitions. One might say that Juárez was a president ahead of his time, and that Díaz governed a country that was trying to modernize itself with methods proper to the preceding century. His protection of the latifundist system made the government's efforts at industrialization unavailing. In the end Díaz' simultaneously brutal and wheedling methods were ineffective, and neither the local caciques nor the científicos could cope with their effects.

The latter must very frequently have felt frustrated by the limitations imposed on them by the agrarian policy of the very president who gave them a share in power, but they did not feel competent to replace Díaz, and feared that some other governing group would promote or accept changes that were too sudden and would upset the public order. For them modernization could be accomplished only in a highly organized and submissive society.

But for all that, the científicos had made strides—with the help of, and at the same time in spite of, Díaz. The growing middle class had come more and more to consider itself indispensable, but Díaz did not take it into account. But as it had no part in government, it felt a sense of frustration. The professionals who were not in the government could do no less than join the opposition. The merchants found their markets limited as much by poverty and oppression in the countryside as by the competition of foreign enterprises and imported articles. The industrialists also feared such competition and wanted the peons to become, some day, the purchasers of their output. And the peasants, naturally, wanted to own land, and to be able to buy the citified things they saw in the houses of the hacendados and caciques. The workers aspired to a higher standard of living, which industry could not give them so long as the peasants could not afford to buy its products.

This contradictory situation did not reveal itself as clearly to the Mexicans at the time as it is described here, because they were blinkered by custom—above all, by the custom of considering the hacienda as a normal element of Mexican society—and by the fear of reprisals by the government and the caciques if they opposed it.

Only the younger men, who had been born and educated when the current order was already in existence, who had not lived under Juárez and his persistent struggle for liberal principles, began to doubt. When the moment came in which the industrial expansion and modernization of the country could go no further, because it had made all the progress it was possible for rural poverty to support and maintain, all these contradictions and frustrations began to bud in the consciousness of the people and to blossom into action.

Díaz and the cientificos did not realize, isolated as they were from the people, that this transformation had taken place in the Mexican mind. If any signs of it reached them, they ascribed what they saw to the influence of "foreign agitators," "exotic ideologies," and "unacknowledgeable personal ambition," and believed that a firm hand, censorship, and a spell in jail would quiet troublemakers. The facts were to show them mistaken.

Díaz had to fight two very fierce Indian wars: he had to crush a rebellion of the Mayas of Yucatán, and overcome a revolt of the Yaquis on the Pacific Coast. Both wars were bloody and were marked by acts of desperation on the part of the Indians as they saw their lands seized and their customs overthrown. There were cases in which, when the men were defeated, the women and their children hurled themselves to death en masse to avoid capture by the federal troops.

These military victories did not dazzle the public, as Díaz thought they would, but fostered opposition to the regime. Books treating the problems of the country from a point of view different from that of the cientificos began to appear. A lawyer, Winstano Luis Orozco, and a professor and lawyer, Andrés Molína Enríquez, wrote about the need of agrarian reform. Molína Enríquez, moreover, pointed out that if Mexico was to become a true nation she would have to emphasize the mestizo nature of the population. The young intellectuals, who saw that the country had made progress—to be sure, chiefly, and almost wholly, in the cities—asked themselves what all this progress had accomplished: the Mexicans now had less liberty and in actual practice did not have the right to elect those who would govern them, as the elections were always skillfully rigged by the caciques. This progress, they said, had been achieved while keeping the mass of Mexicans in a true state of servitude—some in physical servitude, in the rural areas, and others in spiritual servitude, in the cities. Furthermore, that very progress had been financed with foreign capital, especially English and American, and (they reasoned) if the Mexicans continued on the same course they would find themselves no longer the owners of their own country—the arable land, especially, would be in the hands of the Spaniards, and the industry and mines in the hands of the British and the Yankees—and all that would be left for the Mexicans would be the bureaucracy and manual labor.

These young men were reading the works of European and American writers, and it was at this period that native naturalistic novels and symbolist poetry began to be published in Mexico. Intellectually, the country was backward, out of step; and this new generation was impatient to put it in tune with the larger world. The Athenaeum Generation—as the intellectual group, which met at the Ateneo Club in Mexico City, became known—were growing critical of positivism. If science itself was a process of discovery, of questioning, they said, how could the rigidity of positivism be scientific? They took their inspiration especially from French philosopher Henri Bergson's theory of creative evolution. The philosopher Antonio Caso and Alfonso Reyes, a poet and diplomat and the son of General Bernardo Reyes, were outstanding in this group; Caso was the first to interpret Mexico not through foreign doctrines produced in very different societies but through Mexican eyes. By the efforts of this group, the positivists' cultural monopoly was weakened.

And two new parties were to break up the political monopoly of the Porfiristas. The more radical, the Liberal Mexican Party, was launched in 1906 by Ricardo Flores Magón while in exile in Saint Louis, Missouri, with his brothers Jesús and Enrique. Revolutionary in character, the Magonistas' party demanded such important reforms as abolition

Artistic achievement in the service of religion is a mark of Mexican piety, as exemplified by this section of carving from a provincial church door.

of obligatory military service, the establishment of a national guard, nationalization of ecclesiastical property (Díaz had found it advantageous to ease up on the strictures against the Church), and a series of reforms aimed specifically at ending labor exploitation: a minimum wage, an eight-hour day, six-day work week; and a number of health and old-age benefits. Magonista liberals also sought to redress some of the evils perpetrated against the Indians, including a return of communal lands, rural education, and the like. The party leaders worked tirelessly to organize groups of field workers, trade union cells, and to prepare the way for the revolution of city and farm workers which they hoped would someday arise. Responding to their call for change, local clubs appeared, particularly among the textile workers, but also in industrial centers all over Mexico.

The moderate Anti-Re-electionist Party was largely the inspiration of Francisco Madero, an enlightened if eccentric hacendado from the north. The party surfaced in 1909 after Díaz had granted an interview to James Creelman, a reporter for the American journal *Pearson's Magazine,* in which the old dictator had made the startling declaration, "I have waited patiently for the day on which the Mexican people should be prepared to choose and change their government at all times without the danger of war or danger to national credit and progress. I believe the moment has come." And he announced that he would not accept re-election. People did not trust their eyes and ears. Such a thing seemed impossible, although Díaz was seventy-eight years old.

The interview was widely published and it set off a flurry of political activity. Late in that same year Madero published a book entitled *The Presidential Succession of 1910* in which he raised a mild protest against the old regime while paying the necessary respects to Díaz the man. Madero called for a constitutional revision to prevent any more re-elections, for a more effective and honest system of elections, and for the renovation of the administration of government at all levels. Moderate as these proposals were, they caused a sensation. For the first time in a quarter century, an alternative was being offered to those Mexicans who wanted no more of Díaz. Either they could put into power a moderate, democratic president who would not have the means to perpetuate his own incumbency, or they could seek the radical transformation of their society through the Magonistas. But, Díaz' assertions as to his retirement proved to be a sham. When 1910 approached he forgot all about them, announced he was running for a seventh term, and the campaign of pro-Díaz and anti-Díaz forces became a heated one, even though it effectively touched only a small part of the country's inhabitants—the city dwellers—for the peasants were still out of the political picture.

In April, 1910, a convention was held in the Tivoli Theater in Mexico City. At this the Anti-Re-electionist Party proclaimed Madero its candidate. Madero made a stubborn campaign, against strong opposition on the part of the authorities, who arrested him a month before the election on a charge of inciting people to riot during a rally at San Luis Potosí. The elections, held in June, were dirty, violent, and rigged; only 196 votes for Madero were recognized countrywide—fewer votes than there had been delegates to the convention at the Tivoli Theater. On September 16, Mexico City was the scene of a huge celebration of the centennial of the Grito de Dolores, the opening of Mexico's war for independence—and of Díaz' eightieth birthday. To judge from the festivities—bought with 20 million pesos from the federal treasury—the nation had never been more prosperous, more enamored of their leader. But behind this carefully controlled stage show, the furor was mounting.

In October, Madero was released on bail and escaped to Texas. There he declared the elections null and void and announced that he was assuming the provisional presidency of the republic. The document in which he made his declaration is known as the San Luis Potosí Plan, after the city of his imprisonment. In the Plan, November 20 was set as the date on which the Mexicans were to rise in arms against the Díaz dictatorship.

No one knew it, but the Mexican Revolution had begun.

CHAPTER VI

THE MEXICAN
REVOLUTION

Francisco Madero entered Mexico on November 20, 1910, by way of the state of Coahuila, where his hacienda was located. His partisans in the capital and in the city of Puebla had been arrested. Instead of the guerrilla army he had been promised, he was met by no more than twenty-five armed men ready to put themselves under his orders. Discouraged, he returned to the United States and considered giving up his quest. While he was in New Orleans, waiting to take ship for Europe, he got the news that the farmers and ranch hands throughout northern Mexico had formed guerrilla bands. Madero had shown less faith in the Mexican people than they had in him.

A village shopkeeper, Pascual Orozco, and a hacienda peon, Doroteo Arango, who later took the name of Pancho Villa, had organized guerrillas in the border state of Chihuahua, the major part of which was owned by a single family. When news of these events reached the capital, peasant fighters in the neighboring state of Morelos rose in arms under the leadership of a thirty-three-year-old Indian tenant farmer, Emiliano Zapata, and immediately besieged the city of Cuernavaca. Six months later there were guerrillas active all over the country,

A Mexican revolutionary stands firm against the encroaching forces of imperialism in this mural by José Clemente Orozco.

even in Díaz' own state of Oaxaca, and everywhere palls of smoke arose from the hacienda buildings the peasants had set afire. Madero had thought he would be heading a political revolution; now he found that the peasants, eager for lands, were changing it into an agrarian revolution.

The United States, becoming alarmed, sent twenty thousand men toward the frontier. José Yves Limantour, Díaz' secretary of the treasury and now the real head of government, returned from a European diplomatic mission to reorganize the government, sent the most hated politicians abroad, and in April, 1911, began negotiations with Madero. A cease-fire was agreed upon by both sides. The Maderistas demanded Díaz' resignation. Limantour refused to grant this demand. Meanwhile, the guerrilla fighters continued to fight on without orders from anyone at the top. They took Ciudad Juárez on the United States border and Zapata advanced toward the national capital. The irresistible thrust of the guerrilla fighters and the demoralization of the federal forces led to an accord between Limantour and the rebels on May 21. Under its terms, Díaz and Limantour were to resign and the ambassador to Washington, Francisco León de la Barra, was to be provisional president until new elections could be held.

But Díaz, who was ill, refused to resign, and when a large crowd gathered to demonstrate against him, he ordered his troops to fire upon them. Two hundred persons were killed. Finally Díaz' friends, fearing that their houses would be attacked by mobs, persuaded him to yield. The old general resigned on May 25, took the train to Veracruz, and there boarded a German merchant ship. He was to die four years later in Paris, without ever realizing that what was taking place in his country was not a simple matter of rivalries, but a true revolution, the first of the twentieth century, preceding those of Russia and China.

However, Díaz' departure and that of Limantour a week later did not pacify Zapata's guerrillas, who insisted on land as well as liberty. The guerrilla fighters refused to be disbanded but Madero won a conditional bargain with Zapata, who agreed to cease his raids if the candidate would promise to redraw the laws of landownership immediately upon assuming office. Maderistas also had misgivings about the slowness with which their hero was acting, feeling that he ought to demand of the provisional president fulfillment of the San Luis Potosí

Plan. Finally, in October, the election was held. In what was probably the most honest contest ever held in Mexico, Madero won the race for the presidency, and the vice-presidency went to José María Pino Suárez of Yucatán, a man of vaguely socialist leanings.

Now Madero found that he was obliged to do all the things he had not compelled De la Barra's government to do. But he was limited by the threat the army represented, for he had not dared to demand that it be mustered out and replaced by guerrilla forces. Nearly all the military men were Porfiristas and they hoped to force the return of a dictatorship under a mask of constitutionality. An outright coup was impossible for they knew that the people held Madero in the deepest veneration, as a kind of lay saint, and that if any attempt was made against him the guerrillas would rise again. And the guerrillas were better armed than ever. Many fighters, when they went back to their homes, had taken with them the guns captured from the federal forces.

Because he was not a revolutionary, Madero was not inclined temperamentally or philosophically to take dramatic measures, and he was gradually isolated from the people. Zapata lost faith and issued his own program for social change in a document, set down by a schoolteacher associate, known as the Ayala Plan. Convinced that Madero did not intend to bring about a genuine agrarian reform that would give land to the peons, the guerrilla leader resumed his raids. The numerous workers' organizations took advantage of the climate of political freedom to strengthen their position by creating a central Casa del Obrero Mundial (House of World Workers); influenced by anarchist propaganda, they regarded everything as a question of rivalries among members of the bourgeoisie. The adherents of Flores Magón's Liberal Party, who had done so much to weaken Díaz' regime, proclaimed a socialist republic in Baja California, with the aid of members of the American leftist workers' movement, the IWW; they did not propose to separate the peninsula from the rest of the country, but to establish a base there from which pressure could be exerted on Mexico. But the president sent the federal army—that is, the army that had been formed by Díaz—against the liberals and their leaders. The movement was crushed, and they fled to the United States. Ricardo Flores Magón died years later, blind, in the Fort Leavenworth penitentiary, sentenced by the United States for anarchist activities.

Meanwhile, the powerful Terrazas family, which owned nearly six billion acres in Chihuahua state, were furious over Madero's attempt to limit their vast holdings. They bribed the guerrilla leader Pascual Orozco, who had supported Madero in the beginning of the revolution, to raise a revolt against the new government. Prompted by ambition, he declared Madero a "traitor" and led an armed uprising. Orozco's forces were beaten by the federal troops under the command of General Victoriano Huerta, who thus won Madero's grudging trust. (The vegetarian, teetotaling president would continue to be uneasy over Huerta's notorious drinking habits.) Then Félix Díaz, one of Porfirio Díaz' nephews, led an abortive rightist revolt.

Madero's principal demonstration of political courage was in maintaining absolute freedom of speech. The opposition, which with each government crisis became more aggressive, had at its disposal, in addition to the press (for there was not a single Maderista daily), the congress, which had never before functioned with such freedom. The Maderistas sent memoranda and appeals to the president urging him to apply the rest of his original liberal program without any hesitation. But Madero, whose naïveté shielded him from the conspiratorial climate that was overtaking the country, viewed himself as a mediator and conciliator. He was not aware that, with disappointed supporters on one side and with the other side thirsting for revenge, there was nothing to conciliate or reconcile.

Events proved this when it was already too late. From the ninth to the eighteenth of February, 1913, a period known as the Decena Trágica (Ten Tragic Days), several regiments rose in revolt in the capital and freed Generals Bernardo Reyes and Félix Díaz, whose death sentences for rebellion against the government had been commuted by the ever-idealistic Madero. With Reyes now in command, the cadets, aided by the guards, seized the presidential palace. But a group of loyal troops immediately recovered it. In the brief skirmish that ensued when the rebels again tried to seize it, Reyes was killed. Meanwhile, General Félix Díaz captured the citadel and from there resumed the attack on the Palacio Nacional.

Madero rode down on horseback from the castle of Chapultepec, where he lived, to the presidential headquarters. Accompanied by General Huerta, he crossed the city; a crowd, infuriated at the in-

surgent army officers, followed. The American ambassador, Henry Lane Wilson, who had sent his government many dispatches unfavorable to the Madero regime, invited the rebel Félix Díaz and General Huerta to the embassy apparently to negotiate a cease-fire. But the two generals, instead, agreed to work together against Madero and planned the events that soon followed.

On February 18, the palace guards arrested Madero, who was unwilling to believe that Huerta had gone over to the rebels, and Vice-President Pino Suárez. The secretary of state had to assume the presidency, but only for the few minutes needed to name Huerta secretary of the interior and to resign. Huerta automatically became president—all very legally, for the law had established the order of succession among the various secretaries of the government. Gustavo Madero, brother of the deposed president and, in the opinion of many, the real power behind the presidency, was arrested in a restaurant at which he was keeping an appointment with Huerta to negotiate a truce. He was taken to the citadel and tortured to death.

Emiliano Zapata and his followers at the gates of Mexico City, massing in order to drive out the self-appointed President Huerta

The diplomatic corps, having a very low opinion of the hard-drinking Huerta, feared for the lives of Francisco Madero and Pino Suárez. They brought pressure upon the president, who promised to give his captives safe conduct out of the country. Madero's family asked Ambassador Wilson to intercede with Huerta, but the diplomat told them that he could not interfere. To his friends, Lane Wilson expressed the opinion that Madero should be in a lunatic asylum and Pino Suárez should be shot. He certainly did not ask Huerta for clemency. On February 22, the new president ordered his hostages taken from the room in the Palacio Nacional in which they were kept under arrest. It was believed that they were being taken to Veracruz to be deported, but they were taken to the penitentiary and shot against the outside walls, at eleven o'clock that night. An official announcement gave it out that an armed gang had attempted to rescue the prisoners and that in the scuffle they had been killed. But the people immediately suspected, and then learned, the truth. Wilson, however, telegraphed Washington that the official version fit the facts, and the next evening gave a reception at the embassy. For the public, this was tantamount to having the representative of the United States celebrate the assassination of Madero. To this day, to tell a Mexican that he is like Lane Wilson is to deliver him an unforgivable insult.

Huerta remained in office just sixteen months. The confused and intimidated congress had accepted him; Senator Belisario Domínguez, who had made a speech in opposition, was assassinated shortly afterward. When the members of the congress walked out in protest, Huerta ordered a hundred and ten of them arrested and named a new congress, composed almost entirely of army officials and a number of Porfiristas. Huerta's government changed its complexion frequently, for his original supporters were alienated by his brutality. He spent his days not in his office but in saloons, and his nights in cafés, and was nearly always drunk when seen in public.

He decided to call an election, and since he wanted to be elected, he sent Félix Díaz off to Japan, and in doing so he broke the agreement the two had made with Wilson that Díaz was to succeed Huerta. But Huerta did not know his people. He had thought they would be as submissive as they had been earlier. This time, however, the public refused to accept the coup as a *fait accompli,* and they found leaders,

organizers, and agitators to make their will known. If it was true that
Madero had disappointed many people, Huerta had made them realize
that a weak democratic president was better than a strong president
under a dictatorship.

One of those who came around to this viewpoint was the former
Díaz appointee Governor Venustiano Carranza (1859–1920) of Coahuila, Madero's native state. That state's legislature unanimously refused to recognize Huerta, and named Carranza chief of the forces
Coahuila was prepared to raise against the usurper. On March 26,
1913, Carranza and some anti-Huertista colonels and civilians met at
the Hacienda de Guadalupe and approved a plan by the terms of
which they refused recognition to Huerta, his congress, and the governors submissive to him. The Guadalupe Plan also announced the
formation of an army, to be called the "constitutional forces" (whence
his partisans were called *constitucionalistas*), to drive Huerta out and
re-establish respect for the constitution. Carranza was to command this
army, with the title First Chief, and when he moved into the capital
would remain provisional president until an election was held.

In other words, Huerta had to be gotten rid of. But things were
destined to become a great deal more complicated before the issue was
resolved. Carranza had been a minister under Madero and his actions
were guided, above all, by loyalty to the late president. Others wanted
to go beyond the mere restoration of the constitutional system. They
believed that such a system would not be able to function until they had
remedied the fundamental evils of the country—the hacienda system,
and economic dependence on foreign countries. In spite of Carranza,
the constitutional movement thus underwent conversion into a na-
tionalistic and social revolution, the basic causes of which were the
frustration of the middle class and the aspirations of the peasants.

Zapata, who continued to be leader of his peons in the south, contributed greatly to giving the revolution its agrarian content; the
nationalist and libertarian aspects were fostered by the young intellectuals. The sympathy secretly felt for the constitucionalistas by President
Wilson's government (which had succeeded William Howard Taft's
and had promptly recalled the meddling ambassador Lane Wilson)
was of some help in their eventual triumph over Huerta. In this
first stage of the revolution—the struggle against the dictatorship—

the colorful *guerrillero* Pancho Villa became a legendary hero, and other generals emerged. The Mexicans called them *generales de dedo* ("finger generals") because it is said that they were chosen almost at random. Álvaro Obregón and Plutarco Elías Calles were the two who were to achieve the most importance among these makeshift leaders. They were all from the most diverse social classes; Villa was a peon, Obregón a rancher, and Calles an elementary-school teacher.

An idea of the popular reaction at the time may be had from the experience of Villa, who had been put in jail by Huerta while Madero was still in office, and who had escaped into exile in the United States: When he returned, he was accompanied by just eight guerrillas, but within a few weeks, he was at the head of an army of northern Mexicans numbering thousands. Villa and Carranza, both egocentric personalities, did not get along very well, and the governor openly mistrusted the peon. But many intellectuals, impelled by a romantic political concept, admired Villa and served as his advisers. By contrast, Zapata attracted few writers and city men, for they were alarmed at the Indian character of his forces. Zapata's guerrillas did not, properly speaking, form an army; they tilled the soil with their rifles at hand, ready to respond swiftly to the summons of the man the conservatives and the world press had dubbed "the Attila of the South." But Zapata's social ideas, as set forth in the Ayala Plan, were much clearer than Villa's. Perhaps this too contributed to alienating the intellectuals, who saw little chance of influencing Zapata.

Meanwhile, Huerta was steadily losing control of Mexico. Six months after he had seized power, Huerta held only the capital, Veracruz, and a few other cities. To travel through the rest of the country was risky—there were guerrilla bands everywhere and their methods could not always be described as polite or in accord with the laws of war. The films about Villa and Zapata, although not very accurate historically, reflect the outlook and behavior of these infuriated peasants, who found in the course of guerrilla warfare their first shoes, their first rifles, and their first chance to be treated as human beings. They had always been objects of contempt and brutality; therefore, the only things they knew were brutality and contempt.

When Woodrow Wilson had assumed the presidency, he decreed an embargo on the sale of munitions to Mexico and had directed his new

Pancho Villa, the hero of the north, whose cry of "Land and Liberty" inspired legions of peasants to join the revolutionary cause

envoy, John Lind, to try to persuade Huerta to resign. The general, instead, called for elections. When Lind told the Mexican secretary of foreign affairs that Huerta should not be a candidate, the secretary reassured him that Huerta could not legally stand for re-election. And he did not. But after the election, it was announced that the majority of voters had cast their ballots for Huerta anyway; the protest against this farce was so general that finally the dictator declared the election void and he remained in power as provisional president.

President Wilson then lifted the embargo against shipment of arms across the border, thus aiding the constitucionalistas in procuring weapons in their drive against Huerta. In Tampico there was an incident involving the federal troops (Huerta's) and American marines. This gave Wilson an excuse to move against Huerta and in support of Carranza. He sent several ships to blockade Veracruz, toward which was also moving a German ship laden with arms for Huerta. The German government protested, and to avoid direct conflict with Berlin, Wilson ordered the marines to land for a short time in Veracruz, with the intention of preventing the munitions cargo from being unloaded.

The intentions were good, but they revealed the fundamental misunderstanding of the new temper that had been forged in Mexico in the heat of revolution. Although Wilson's order was favorable to the constitucionalistas, the latter protested the marines' landing as a violation of the national territory, and some constitucionalistas in the port joined Huerta's troops in the struggle against the Americans. Then Huerta, who had succeeded in getting the German arms via another port, and the constitucionalistas, who had armed themselves hurriedly with American equipment, returned to fighting one another. Finally, Huerta, seeing that his forces were all but lost, resigned on July 15, 1914, and went abroad. A month later, after negotiations with the president of the supreme court acting as provisional president, Obregón entered the capital at the head of the constitutional forces.

The people of the city took a deep breath of relief. They thought the revolution was over. But the hardest part was still to come, for the expressions Villista and Carranzista were already current, and the constitutionalist camp divided. The strain had become apparent as the armies converged on Mexico City; Villa's cavalry proceeding, often by train, down the central plateau and Obregón's men marching down the

Pacific Coast. Carranza had forbidden Villa to take the central Mexican city of Zacatecas, apparently in a move to deny him another prestigious victory, but Villa stormed it anyway. Then Carranza cut off further supplies of coal to fuel Villa's trains, thereby assuring Obregón the glory of taking the capital. On the political front, Zapata was demanding that, instead of Carranza's moderate Guadalupe Plan, his Ayala Plan should be adopted. His plan was equally moderate in tone, but more sweeping in relation to the agrarian question. Like many others who had been disappointed by Madero's political timidity, he was distrustful of Carranza, fearing that he would also be a disappointment. The fact that many Porfiristas, when they saw that everything was lost, had turned to him in the hope that he would impose order and restore tranquillity without making any radical changes also served to undermine the Villistas' confidence.

Carranza, in an effort to bring unity to the revolutionary forces and assure his election as president, called a convention in Mexico City, but the rival Villista and Zapatista factions forced its removal to Aguascalientes, a railroad center within the territory under Villa's control. Carranza consequently boycotted the meeting and there, on October 10, 1914, with representatives of all the revolutionary groups present, it was agreed that Carranza would cease to be First Chief and that Villa would no longer be chief of the North Division.

The convention chose as interim president General Eulalio Gutiérrez. But Carranza refused to give up his post, and as the capital was garrisoned by forces under a general who was a Villa sympathizer and for the moment at least a supporter of the Gutiérrez compromise, he went with his government to Veracruz. Gutiérrez went to Mexico City. And on the first of January, 1915, Zapata and Villa, at the head of their respective armies—some fifty thousand in all—entered the capital. The citizens feared for the worst, especially from the Indians. As they soon discovered, Zapata's men were far from fierce; rather, these tattered soldiers, none of them in uniform, went from house to house with machetes in their belts and carbines on their shoulders, humbly asking for something to eat and drink. Villa's Dorados from the north were much less disciplined and made a reputation for themselves as brawling drunkards and pillagers.

So now there were two governments: the moderate constitutionalist

VILLA EN LA SILLA PRESIDENCIAL   CASASOLA=FOT   No 6.

one at Córdoba and the more radical one formed at the convention and now installed in Mexico City. Carranza continued Obregón as chief of his forces and Gutiérrez, who really had no choice, accepted Villa as the head of his. However, Villa's forces were not strong enough to hold the reactionary capital, and for this reason the Gutiérrez government removed to San Luis Potosí. There Gutiérrez was replaced by a civilian. Finally, the convention government, still bickering, fell apart.

Villa and Zapata continued their fight against Carranza. When they had first met in Mexico City, there had been a natural easiness between them. Standing before the gilt presidential chair, Villa invited Zapata to sit down in it. Zapata replied, "It would be better to burn it, for I have seen that everybody who has sat in this chair has become an enemy of the people."

However, good intentions not withstanding, they did not manage to coordinate their activities and operations. With their government collapsed and Carranza's forces restored to strength, Zapata and his demoralized troops returned to their hacienda war in the south and Villa

The victorious Pancho Villa, surrounded by his followers, poses uneasily in the presidential chair with a wary Emiliano Zapata beside him.

to the great spaces of the north, where the trains went great distances without stopping and horse-mounted guerrillas galloped at will.

In the meantime, Obregón had made contact with the leaders of the Casa del Obrero Mundial. Until then, the industrial workers had not taken part in the revolution—at least, not as an organized group—because their anarchistic leanings led them to view the conflict as a capitalist affair. But Obregón convinced them that, if they wanted to derive any benefit from the revolution, they could not remain outside it, but must participate.

Obregón did not merely want to win the unions to the constitutionalist cause, but also wanted to attract them to his own cause in the struggle he foresaw with his leader Carranza. Zapata and Villa, when they were in Mexico City, had made no attempt to ally themselves with the unions, despite what would appear to be their mutual interests. Their peasant outlook made them wary of the city workers, and the latter, for their part, considered the armed peons little better than savages. This, most likely, was what decided the struggle in Carranza's favor. For the Casa del Obrero Mundial began to organize "red battalions" (which proved very efficient) after they had signed a pact with Carranza in Veracruz, in which the unions were committed to support Carranza in return for social legislation that would protect the workers.

Meanwhile, Obregón had continued to win battles from the Villistas. He recaptured Puebla and Guadalajara, and finally a decisive battle was fought before the city of Celaya, with 20,000 constitucionalistas against 25,000 Villistas. Villa was routed. By the end of 1915 there were no more organized Villista forces, but only scattered and fleeing bands. Villa himself took refuge in the plains of Chihuahua, and held out there for a while.

But Zapata was still to be reckoned with. His resistance lasted until 1919. In the end he was betrayed and assassinated: a Carranzista colonel offered to join his side and an interview was arranged. When Zapata arrived for the meeting, he was riddled by fire from a hidden group of Carranzista soldiers. The colonel who had arranged the assassination received a reward of 50,000 pesos and was made a general.

The early military successes of the revolution could be traced ultimately to Zapata. From the beginning the people in the capital had been so fearful of attack by the Zapatistas that large garrisons were kept concentrated there, leaving the federal army, first under Díaz and then under Huerta, weakened and without a secure rear guard. Zapata, with his great drooping mustaches and his cold eyes, inspired fear, but did not commit any acts of great cruelty. Villa, on the other hand, with his swashbuckler airs and loud laugh, was a more winning personality, but this did not prevent his conducting himself with great brutality. The differences of character between the two *caudillos* (strong men) and their mutual inability to consider their activity as an affair of the entire country ultimately cost them the political victory.

Carranza, aided as he was by Obregón's military intuition, slowly regained the upper hand. Even before the assassination of Zapata the constitucionalistas could call themselves masters of the entire country. They began to plan for the future, first of all by satisfying current aspirations. While Zapatistas and Villistas were handing out land without bothering about law, the Carranza government, in 1915, passed a measure ordering civilian and military authorities to give ejidos to the villages that were demanding them; owners of lands thus expropriated were permitted to appeal to the courts within a year. A National Agrarian Commission was created to enforce this law, and it was emphasized that if an expropriation was declared illegal by the courts, the government would compensate the owner, but without taking the land back from the peasant to whom it had been given.

This law represented the norm of all agrarian Mexican reform. Like many other of Carranza's actions, it was the work of Luis Cabrera, a lawyer who had early tried unsuccessfully to persuade Madero to have a similar law passed. As Cabrera himself explained, he had conceived the ejido as a kind of school for future proprietors—a transitory institution—since the great majority of the peasants who were going to receive land had never owned any. By this device he hoped to avoid the exploitation to which an earlier generation of Indian landowners had been exposed when they had received land under the Reform Laws of 1857—that is, being pressured into selling their new property for a fraction of its worth or having it taken away through legalized chicanery. The objective of the law was not to perpetuate the ejido system but to create a class of rural farm owners of small and medium-sized holdings. However, it was impossible to prevent many of the "finger

generals" from taking possession of large tracts and forming new
haciendas. Villa himself acquired a middle-sized hacienda for his retirement; in 1923 he was assassinated by a resentful local proprietor.

Nevertheless, the fact of owning lands did not mean, as it had under
Díaz, the automatic possession of political power. This now belonged
to the middle class, from which most of the constitutionalist leaders
had come. As the peasants had undergone military defeat, and as the
workers had not taken part in the struggle until somewhat later, the
two forces that might have been able to demand power were thrust
aside. The middle-class leaders realized, however, that without satisfying these two forces no government could expect any stability. For
this reason, they passed various laws in favor of the workers, establishing the right to organize unions and suppressing company stores.
Divorce was also permitted.

In the meantime, in Yucatán, the revolutionary general and governor, Salvador Alvarado, an ardent socialist, had codified a series of
innovative social laws for his state in 1915—and used state funds to
form workers' Ligas de Resistencia, socialist pressure groups. As the
peninsula's almost exclusive source of income was henequen (sisal),
he created a Comision Reguladora del Mercado de Henequen (Regula-
tory Commission of the Henequen Market), which was really a body
for planning and commercializing its cultivation and for overseeing the
maintenance of high prices in foreign markets. Alvarado organized
henequen ejidos into cooperatives, extended credits to the building of
mills to process the crop, and set up departments to promote the economic development of Yucatán; then the local railroad was acquired
and a number of public works financed. The progressive governor decreed that there should be a school in every ejido, and loans were offered for their construction. Alvarado wanted to go further, and he
promulgated an agrarian law which affirmed that "no one is the exclusive owner of land, any more than of light and air." There were so
many protests that Carranza annulled the legislation. Similarly, other
governors were creating new laws and policies to govern their own
states, a situation which threatened to fragment revolutionary Mexico
if they were not brought under firm central control. Carranza, following the advice of friends, decided to consolidate the laws by reforming
the constitution of 1857.

The country was almost wholly peaceful. The United States had recognized the Carranza government, cutting off Villa's arms supply from across the U.S.-Mexican border, and when Villa, in a fit of rage, had attacked the American frontier city of Columbus, New Mexico, General "Black Jack" Pershing had been sent in to pursue him. When Pershing entered Mexican territory in March, 1916, Carranza protested violation of its borders and, after various encounters with Villistas and Carranzistas, the American forces withdrew without capturing Villa.

Moreover, the failure of Pershing's expedition, and the fact that the constitucionalistas had opposed it in spite of its being directed at their rivals (just as they had when the U.S. Marines had tangled with Huerta in Veracruz in 1914), reinforced Carranza's prestige. Now the time seemed propitious for an election to seat a constituent congress. He denied the right of being elected to those who had in one way or another supported Huerta.

The congress convened on the first of December, 1916, in a theater in the city of Querétaro, and at the end of ten weeks declared its work complete. On the right were those who had been adherents of Madero; the center was formed by the constitucionalistas or Carranzistas, and the left by socialists, some Zapata partisans, and some union members.

Villistas, wounded but still game, pose above; more severe casualties are nursed by friends and camp followers along a railroad track (above right).

The center had an absolute majority, but within it there were sympathizers with both right and left.

Carranza had expected the congress simply to reform the old constitution. But the congress drafted a new constitution, which gave Mexico a republican federal regime modeled on the American one. At that time Mexico had 27 states and 5 territories. (Today she has 29 states and 2 territories.) The constitution, besides, established the usual guarantees of civil rights; it provided for elections, forbade the reelection of president and legislature, and strengthened the system of habeas corpus known as the law of amparo.

Three articles were the subject of long debate, but, once approved, they gave the constitution its character. Article 3 proclaimed freedom of education; it made public education lay-controlled and free, and forbade the Church to have schools of its own. Article 27 declared that ownership of lands and waters was vested in the nation, which had the right to expropriate land whenever the interests of society so dictated. Society presumably demanded that land be redistributed to give the peasants a fair share. Here the debates followed an old Spanish juristic pattern that had been applied in the colony. The peasants had the right to demand return of lands and waters of which they had been de-

spoiled. But perhaps the most important feature of this article was that it declared the subsoil—that is, the mines—national and inalienable property, reversing the costly policy of the Díaz regime. This article was approved on the last day of the congress, and by candlelight, as there had been a power failure.

Finally, Article 123 proclaimed in full detail the right of workers to organize into unions and to call strikes, and the proceedings by which the state would act as arbitrator in labor conflicts. This article also established the principle of equal pay for equal work, and the eight-hour day; it forbade anyone under twelve years of age to work, it provided a Sunday holiday, and it set up a mechanism for periodical determination of a minimum wage. Moreover, the article recognized the right of workers to share in the profits of industry. It is very likely that the Mexican constitution is the only one in the world that, instead of setting up only a few general principles concerning the rights of labor, spells out these rights. This was achieved by the union member deputies after many maneuvers and much discussion, for they were

Patriots with the misfortune of being on the losing side await execution.

cynical enough to anticipate that, when it came to enforcing the constitution, a way would be found to evade enforcement of these rights unless a procedure for making them effective had been established in the constitution itself.

The document was approved and promulgated on February 5, 1917. It is still in force in Mexico and is one of the longest-lived Latin-American constitutions. Although only a very small number of representatives of the peasants and the workers were present at its drafting, the constituent deputies took the aspirations of these two social sectors into consideration, for they knew, as has been said, that otherwise there could be no stability for the new regime. But the fact that the workers had not taken part in the revolution, and so could not present a bill for their support of it, gave the constitution a tutelary character; rights for the peasants and workers, surely, but granted by the middle class, which was to have the responsibility for seeing that the rights were respected to the degree it saw fit. Obviously this was not explicitly stated, but it was tacitly understood that the middle class would do the governing and would therefore be responsible for enforcement of the constitution.

So the middle class was, de facto, in charge of governing the country. It saw itself as exercising a regency for the peasants and workers, for their own benefit, presumably because they were not capable of doing it for themselves. The brutalities of the agrarian rebellion and labor's indifference to the revolution until it was well advanced seemed to the middle class a proof that the great mass of the population was not prepared to govern. For the idealistic, the mission of the middle class was to prepare the masses for a role in government; for the more pragmatic, it consisted in profiting by this lack of preparation to keep the direction of government as its own privilege, though at the same time, satisfying the lower classes.

And so the revolution, which had begun as a merely political one intended to prevent the re-election of Díaz, had passed through various phases. In each phase it added a new feature, with the result that it ended up by being a many-faceted revolution, with a political aspect (the establishment of a democracy), a social aspect (the rights of the peasants and workers), and a nationalist aspect (national ownership of the subsoil).

There were many active forces that would make moving from the

OVERLEAF: *Portraits of both heroes and villains of the revolution appear in Diego Rivera's mural entitled "Impassioned Documentary."*

letter of the constitution to its enforcement a hard, complex, and at times bloody task. Although the revolution had destroyed the obstacles in the way of Mexico's being converted into a democracy, giving land to the peasants and affirming her economic independence, it still remained to discover permanent solutions to the problems the revolution had raised.

The ills to be remedied had been increased by the revolution, at the same time as it had created conditions for their cure. For the first time, Mexico had had a civil war that was not a mere military exercise of small armed groups but which had mobilized great masses of men. The hacendados had disappeared, but in their place had arisen the newly rich of the revolution—speculators and ambitious "finger generals" converted into big landholders. Productive haciendas had been burned down in great numbers. The new owners of the land had no experience in making agricultural decisions or in cultivating the land for themselves.

Many industries had been paralyzed by the conflict; many merchants and industrialists had left the country, taking their money with them. There were no new investments from abroad, for outside Mexico the revolution was viewed as an almost Bolshevik affair, and this belief was strengthened by the propaganda of the émigrés whose interests had been injured by it. The extensive foreign interests that had survived the holocaust, respected by the revolution for diplomatic reasons, were now fearful for their extensive agricultural lands, their oil fields, and their mines, and pressured the government directly and through their national embassies. There was the Church, which had steadfastly opposed the revolution—although many priests in villages and hamlets supported it—and around which all the survivors of the old regime congregated. The Church was particularly disturbed by the clause in Article 3 providing lay teaching and prohibiting religious schools.

Troubles persisted on the left, as well. The assassination of Zapata had decapitated the agrarian movement, but had not destroyed it. Peasant guerrillas still fought in various places, and an Agrarian Party was founded in Mexico City to defend Zapata's ideals and to extend them beyond the state of Morelos that they might assume national dimensions. The workers, when they realized that they had got aboard too late to take a leading role in the revolution, were trying to recover lost ground by strengthening their unions and taking maximum advantage of the rights the constitution gave them. The labor groups that supported Carranza and were committed to close cooperation with the government organized a Laborista Party and their own union federation, the CROM (Confederación Regional Obrera Mexicana, or Regional Mexican Workers' Confederation); those who had remained faithful to anarchist ideals and who were reviving the memory of Flores Magón organized the CGT (Confederación General del Trabajo, or General Labor Confederation), which favored direct action rather than government intervention allegedly on its behalf when labor's interests were threatened. Added to these challenges to governmental order was the challenge of mobilizing the people to begin the rebuilding of Mexico. The population of the country had been literally almost decimated. Including those killed in battle, executed, and dead of causes involved with the revolution (starvation, lack of medical care, and so on) in the seven years from Madero's unseating of Díaz to the ratification of the constitution of 1917, it has been calculated that nearly a million persons perished. Mexico's population at the time did not exceed fifteen million, which means that one out of fifteen Mexicans was snatched from among the living by the agonies of civil war.

Moreover, there remained many hatreds, distrusts, and resentments; between Villistas and Carranzistas, Zapatistas and Carranzistas, between revolutionaries and Porfiristas, the clergy and laity, the people of the city and the people of the country, between rich and poor, the educated and the illiterate, and as always between whites and mestizos and Indians. To blend all these contrary interests, overcoming rivalries, memories, and resentments, to guide all efforts toward solution of the national ills, was the first task of the victors. Now it would be seen if the revolution had served any purpose.

CHAPTER VII

ERA OF THE
FINGER GENERALS

From the very beginning of the colonial era, there had been in
Mexico a slow, hesitant, scarcely ever conscious formation of what we
call nationality. During the years of the colony this process was chiefly
biological, one of the mingling of the two races. The country was
changing into a nation to the degree in which its population was being
integrated into a predominant human type—the mestizo. After independence the evolution was mostly political, a process of searching for
—and sometimes finding—special ways of governing and exercising
power. The revolution greatly accelerated the process. Mexico's social
classes were entering the long road toward integration via the middle
class—urban as well as rural. And this was fostered equally by agrarian
reform, nationalization of the subsoil, and the governmental protection
given to labor.

All these, however, were matters of legality. They had to be transformed into daily practice, into tangible reality. This was the task
undertaken, often almost spontaneously and involuntarily, by a succession of governments we would call revolutionary; that is to say,
formed by men who had come out of the revolution, who owed their

*In "Battle for Liberty," José Clemente Orozco expressed the passionate willing-
ness of his countrymen to fight against all odds for independence.*

political personality and moral authority to it, and who had taken part in it. These men set themselves to making a nation out of a country—which meant to give common interest, culture, and aspirations to all the ethnic and social groups of Mexico. The intellectuals, who had had intuitions of this mission, continued to bend their efforts to those ends, and little by little even the least cultivated segments of the population began to embrace the idea of nationhood.

The revolutionary executives all had certain traits in common, despite many differences in personality. Most had been "finger generals," thrust into responsibility in revolutionary battle, who did not consider themselves professional officers beyond the degree that being an officer gave them influence in the army and a livelihood. When the revolution ended, Mexico had a surplus of such officers, all the more obvious in that the guerrillas and soldiers were rapidly mustered out and there were only a few men left under the command of each leader. This reduction of forces was a foresighted measure taken by Carranza, in the hope of lessening the risk of military coups.

Another thing about the new generation of leaders was that, whatever had been their ideological beginnings, in nearly every case they came under the influence of quite possibly the greatest political figure produced by the revolution—General Plutarco Elías Calles. A schoolteacher before he joined the struggle, Calles was dry and humorless, decisive, a good administrator, and by no means hostile to the notion of becoming rich. But when it suited him he manifested a brutality born of seven years of fighting. Calles' historical perspective and sense of the future was sufficient to take him out of the class of simple politician and put him in the category of statesman. In the history of Mexico, only Morelos and Juárez can be compared to him.

In 1917, after the constitution had been ratified, it did not seem that Calles was destined to play a major role. He was one of the most respected and feared of the Carranzistas, but other figures were more impressive. Calles, like other politicians and soldiers who had come out of the revolution, believed sincerely that the constitution ought to be more than a mere symbolic paper; he wanted to see it become a touchstone of Mexican policy accepted as fact rather than as a description of national aspirations.

Carranza, occupying the presidency by vote of the constituent congress, was not similarly motivated. The constitution which he was given to administer seemed to him the product of the rather wild dreams of radicals, and he regarded himself not so much as a man charged with doing all he could to transform the document from paper to reality but rather as one responsible for adapting the constitution to what he thought were the realities of the country's situation. For him, the revolution had triumphed with the fall of Huerta; the rest had been a struggle to keep this outcome from being used to change the country radically, which now suited him just as it was.

Once legally and definitely in the presidency, he turned his chief attention to reorganizing the administrative machinery in such a way that it would take exclusive charge of enforcing the constitution. He took a mistrustful view of the peasant leagues, the unions, even the political parties, and indeed any instrument of pressure. He nationalized the haciendas—which was easy to do, as most of the owners had left the country—and his National Agrarian Commission set to distributing lands wherever the demand for them might conduce to disorder if unfulfilled. Still it was a cautious policy. The governors, who were closer to the people and more radical than the federal government, saw this program as depriving them of one of the strongest tools of their office, since all good things were to come from the central power. During Carranza's term only 450,000 acres of land were given out to some 50,000 families, an insignificant amount considering the number of landless people.

And while he was checking agrarian reform, Carranza came into conflict with the labor movement. The revolution had caused a tremendous inflation. Gold and silver money, hitherto in common use, was no longer in circulation, and many local governments had issued paper money to deal with the expenses of war. While Carranza was putting the treasury in order the workers were finding that their wages, inadequate to begin with, were worth less each day. The unions in the capital declared a general strike, demanding higher pay. Carranza shut down the Casa del Obrero Mundial, ordered many arrests, and had the union leader Luis Morones condemned to death. Álvaro Obregón, who had remained on the periphery of power since the revolution, and had several years before brought the Casa del Obrero Mundial over to the Carranzista side, managed to have Morones' sentence commuted to imprisonment. In Tampico, the organizer of the oil workers was assassinated. The world-wide influenza epidemic, which reached Mexico at the end of 1918, made the already poor situation of the workers still worse, for no system for the provision of special medical care was available to them.

Carranza succeeded in stifling the inflation, and gold and silver money began to circulate again, but little of it ever reached the workers and still less reached the peasants. What good had the revolution done, then? The Catholics began to reorganize—that is, the Conservative Party reappeared. Nuclei of workers known as CROM, directed by the so-called Grupo Acción (Action Group) that had rallied around Morones, formed a Labor Party which proposed to present Obregón as its candidate for president in the 1920 elections. But Obregón was *persona non grata* to Carranza; the latter had put forward as his party's candidate the Mexican ambassador to the United States, a man unknown to the country at large and with very poor revolutionary credentials. In the army, where memories of the long struggle were still bright, this caused widespread dissatisfaction. Nevertheless, Carranza, with all the apparatus of government to back his candidate, had a good chance of winning.

In April of 1920 the railroad workers in Obregón's home state of Sonora struck, and Carranza sent troops to put down the strike. Obregón then decided to act. His friend Governor Adolfo de la Huerta (no relation to Victoriano Huerta) proclaimed the state's independence, and Calles, commander of its forces, published the Agua Prieta Plan, which announced opposition to the continuance in office of Carranza or his personal appointee and to his conservative policy. It asked that he resign and name a provisional president who would assure fair elections. Obregón, who was in the capital, escaped to Sonora when Carranza sent the police to arrest him.

Calles, who enjoyed great popular prestige, led a small force toward Mexico City. On the way he picked up garrisons and former guerrillas who took their rifles and ammunition out of their hiding places. Seeing that he was deserted, Carranza pocketed part of the federal treasury and went off to the coast. His train was attacked by troops of the governor of Veracruz, and Carranza fled to the mountains on horseback. While he was sleeping in the village of Tlaxcalantongo he was mur-

Even as late as the Diaz regime, half of Mexico's babies died in infancy. The bitterness of this birthright is captured here by David Alfaro Siqueiros.

dered by the local cacique, who announced that Carranza had committed suicide.

With the Obregonistas now in the capital, Governor De la Huerta was proclaimed provisional president. He called an election in November, 1920, and Álvaro Obregón was the winner. De la Huerta, to attract the Zapatistas, reconfirmed the legality of all the seizures of lands made up to that time, and Jesús Guajardo, the man who had assassinated Zapata, was tried and executed.

Obregón, a former rancher and smalltime merchant who had lost an arm as the result of wounds incurred in the revolution, was a large man with great mustaches and a jovial sense of humor. He always wore a military jacket, but without braid or medals. With the consent and the steady backing of Calles, he organized his government around several former revolutionaries and some young intellectuals. One of these, José Vasconcelos, became secretary of education. He reorganized teaching practices, initiated a plan for the construction of schools and the training of teachers, and created school missions, which carried books, films, exhibitions, and theatrical presentations to the villages. He founded special schools for the Indians, modernized the university, and arranged for Diego Rivera, José Clemente Orozco, and David Alfaro Siqueiros to paint frescoes on many public buildings.

The works of these muralists marked the rebirth of an art form that had an ancient heritage in Mexico; in their painting they sought a didactic expression that would educate the masses politically and be within their intellectual grasp—for this reason they rejected easel painting as an elitist occupation patronized by the rich. Both Siqueiros and Rivera became communists; the latter was a Trotskyite and was host to Trotsky in his home in 1940. Siqueiros, a Stalinist, organized and took part in an unsuccessful attempt on the life of the Bolshevik leader. (It was because of this failure that the Russian political police decided to have Trotsky liquidated by one of their own agents.)

Obregón and Calles had a crude, almost schematic plan for transforming Mexico into a capitalistic society which, in their minds, was the goal of the revolution. Capitalism presupposed the existence of a rural middle class, to which end the distribution of lands was to continue, and of a relatively satisfied working class with a decent standard of living. This was not something that could be accomplished in a few

years. It would require several successive presidents following the same
policy. A capitalistic society also required political parties, an active
parliament, and an army under civilian control. The parties emerged
soon enough—the Agrarian Party, the Labor Party already mentioned,
the Cooperative Party, and a rightist Catholic group, besides the Communist Party just established in 1921. In congress, and especially in
the press, there was free criticism of Obregón's government. This did
not keep the president from exiling his rivals or having them assassinated, which Obregón did in some cases, but he did so without limiting
the freedom of the press or intimidating congress. Obregón depended
chiefly on the support of the unions of the CROM under the leadership
of Morones and on the Ligas Campesinas (Peasant Leagues).

His policies encountered two obstacles: the opposition of the
Church, the expropriated hacendados, and other groups; and the
greed of many "finger generals" who, not content with the haciendas
they had created for themselves, tried to make big, fast, and dubious
deals. Obregón disdained such opposition, especially that of the "finger
generals," whom he was accustomed to pacifying by throwing a bone
in the form of crooked business or a benefice. As he liked to say of
these lapsed heroes, "There isn't a one who can stand up to a cannonade
of twenty-five thousand pesos."

Obregón announced that he would distribute more land to the peasants, taking it away from such latifundists as were still in existence, but
always with safeguards against the diminution of agricultural production. When many people, attracted by aspects of the Russian Revolution, had declared themselves in favor of communal property, Obregón
moved to offset the trend by passing a law in 1923 which gave a parcel
of land to each member of an ejido as his private property. This did not
include the right to sell it—for Obregón wanted to establish a system
of "common property in private use and guarantee the peasant the
enjoyment of the entire product of the investment of his labor or
capital." The agrarians supported this law enthusiastically. There were
still a million peons working on someone else's property for a wage—
and there were violent encounters in the rural areas between bands of
peons and the authorities. The great landholders refused to accept the
agrarian reform bonds the government gave them as compensation for
expropriated lands—bonds that yielded a moderate rate of interest,

could be used to pay taxes, and were redeemable in twenty years. The expropriations nevertheless went on, and this compelled many latifundists to redirect their investments to industry. In this way, agrarian reform indirectly contributed to the country's industrialization as well.

About three million acres were distributed to 624 villages during Obregón's presidency. But 320 million acres were still in the possession of the great landholders, and in view of these figures, there began to be talk of the "failure" of agrarian reform.

As Obregón's chief urban support came from the unions of the CROM, the government favored its union allies by strict enforcement of the labor laws. For a strike to be declared legal, all means of conciliation had to be exhausted. As this mediation was effected by boards of arbitration presided over by a government appointee, it was easy for the government to declare legal all strikes called by the CROM, and to declare illegal all those organized by other labor federations. Although this provoked bloody rivalries in the bosom of the labor movement, it did somewhat improve the material conditions of the workers through the strikes won by the CROM's unions.

The CROM did not want to destroy capitalism but to make it possible for the workers to share the profits of capitalism. However, this position did not satisfy everybody. Besides the anarchosyndicalist CGT, which despite the government's prejudiced opposition continued to grow, a series of socialist groups and parties arose, all aspiring to a rapid changeover of the country's budding capitalism to some form of socialist organization. For instance, there was a Southeastern Socialist Party organized by Yucatán's General Salvador Alvarado; this later was changed into the Yucatán Resistance Leagues, led by Felipe Carrillo Puerto, who also became governor of the state. The party had the collaboration of the American IWW leader Robert Haberman. There was also a Radical Socialist Party in Tabasco, headed by Tomás Garrido Canabal, which was aggressively anticlerical. The Mexican Communist Party was organized during this same period through the initiative of Manabrenda Nath Roy, a Hindu from India, who had taken refuge in Mexico (and who was later expelled by the Communist International); the party also received indoctrination from the Japanese Sen Katayama and the Russian Mikhail Borodin, sent by the Third International to fortify the newborn Latin-American communist

A thatched adobe hut, a direct descendant of houses that have sheltered peasants since ancient times, is shown here in Kabah, Yucatán.

parties. The Communist Party did not win much influence over the masses in Mexico, but it did enlist a number of intellectuals and artists, among them the muralists Rivera and Siqueiros. The different Socialist parties were independent on the international level, whereas the Communist Party was affiliated with the Third International. The CROM, for its part, collaborated with the American Federation of Labor in 1919 to form the COPA (Confederación Obrera Panamericana, or Pan-America Federation of Labor). Though it had little influence on Latin America and lasted only until 1930, COPA did exert considerable pressure on Washington in defense of the Mexican Revolution, which a good part of the American press continued to brand "red" and "communist" and to hold up as a menace to the United States.

In Washington the Republican president, Warren Harding, lent a willing ear to the oil companies (actually American holdings in Mexico were considerably smaller than British oil properties). All the oil firms were disturbed by Article 27 of the constitution, which belatedly gave Mexico ownership of the resources of the subsoil, including naturally, oil. Obregón knew that if this article were enforced conflicts would arise not only with the foreign firms, but also with the governments of the countries to which they belonged. He contented himself with imposing a number of new taxes, which the companies described as "confiscatory," although they were smaller than the taxes some of the same companies paid in the United States.

Washington did not understand that many of the Mexican government's declarations were radical in expression only to pacify, verbally, its leftist allies. So Washington waited two years after Obregón took office to recognize his government. Finally, Obregón declared that Article 27 was not retroactive and that consequently it would not apply to foreign firms established in Mexico before 1917, when the new constitution was ratified. Washington then made the tactless mistake of demanding that the declaration be embodied in a treaty, and Obregón refused, for he considered doubting the word of the president of the country an insult. Finally, in August, 1922, the Mexican government was recognized by Washington. A commission was set up to indemnify foreign citizens whose property had been jeopardized by the revolution. In 1934, when the commission ceased to function, it had paid out 5.5 million dollars.

The regime had run worse risks than the one Harding's administration presented. Calles was minister of the interior, and everyone thought of him as the candidate to succeed Obregón. But Adolfo de la Huerta, when he had been provisional president for a few months, had developed a taste for power, and now presented himself as Calles' opponent. Realizing that he would be defeated in the election, he organized a coup in December, 1923. Two generals led armed uprisings, one in Veracruz and another in Guadalajara. They operated in the way they had learned during the revolution—by jailing and executing a number of officials, among them Carrillo Puerto, governor of Yucatán. Being in control there for some weeks, they made the mistake of taking land away from the peasants and returning it to the former hacendados. This brought about the rising of many peasant bands. Obregón bought arms in the United States, without interference from Washington, where it doubtless was the opinion that a revolutionary like Obregón, with whom it had reached an accord, was better than just a revolutionary-adventurer. Peasants armed with American equipment, and aided by a few troops, put an end to the uprising after a

President-elect Álvaro Obregón converses with a companion on his left at a celebration luncheon just five minutes before his assassination.

three-month struggle. De la Huerta fled to the United States. The government emerged from the crisis stronger than before, and Calles was elected president in July, 1924. Obregón suspended 54 "finger generals" and replaced them with a like number of younger men from the officer ranks. But the era of coups and armed struggle had not yet ended.

After his election, Calles encountered two situations fraught with the greatest danger. If he had not been such a skillful politician he would probably have been ruined. He governed with the collaboration of Obregón, who was for him what Calles had been for Obregón himself—a moderating influence. Calles was at once progressive and tough. He adopted measures that solidified the foundation of the country's progress, and he made use of violent means, including the *ley fuga* (shooting arrested men under the pretense that they were trying to escape), to enforce his programs.

Although he sometimes referred to himself as a socialist, his policies tended more and more to the right as years passed and his power grew. And his power did grow—during his four-year term and on into the thirties, as he hand-picked his puppet successors and directed their governments. For twelve years—until Lázaro Cárdenas rebelled in 1936, the presidency was effectively a Calles monopoly. Despite the allotment of one fourth of the federal budget to the army for the purpose of keeping it quiet, many schools, roads, and other public works were constructed; industries were created, often with indirect federal aid; and Calles effected some improvement in the workers' condition. Lands were distributed in great quantities—eight million acres to fifteen hundred communes in the four years of his presidency. To prevent abuse of the peasants, especially by the bureaucrats, in 1927 he had passed the Ejidal Patrimony Law, which declared that any land received from the state could not be resold. Furthermore, he encouraged small and medium-sized properties and established a bank for agricultural loans. There was corruption, and many politicians and high officials got rich, but as they invested the product of their abuses in the country, this too contributed to its progress.

To carry out his policies, Calles had the aid not only of Obregón and the Obregonista officers—old revolutionary comrades in arms— but also of the Zapatistas and of the CROM, which had a million industrial workers and half a million peasants in its rank and file, although not 5 per cent of them paid union dues. He had also the backing of a part of the middle class, especially that part that had risen in the world and derived its well-being from governmental policies.

Two major forces were opposed to Calles and his supporters. One was made up of Carranzista officers, moderates, who thought Calles was going too far in his relations with the labor movement and the distribution of land. The other chief obstacle remaining was the Church, which was still not resigned to losing its influence on education and was always fearful lest, some day, Article 3 of the constitution would be strictly enforced. Obregón, and after him Calles, did not enforce it because they did not want to arouse the Catholics, but the Article, with its potential threat, was there. The Church leaders, however, had a mistaken notion about the state of mind of the faithful. If the whites and the rich among them were opposed to the revolution, the mestizos and the Indians remained its most devoted supporters, sermons not withstanding. The priests, in 1921, tried to organize unions to oppose the CROM and failed, despite their declaration that to belong to the CROM was a mortal sin. Isolated, thus, from the people—although the majority continued to hear mass and to consider themselves Catholics—the Church drew nearer and nearer to the former Porfiristas and Carranzistas. In 1926, when certain acts of brutality on the part of the police had alienated the intellectuals and students, and the middle class had become restless, the Church thought the moment had come for action. In this it had the backing of the press.

The bishops had, in 1917, drafted a letter of protest against the newly approved constitution, particularly against the accursed Article 3. They decided to republish the letter in 1926, and sent copies to the newspapers, all of which printed it. Calles regarded this letter as a provocative act and his immediate response was the deportation of foreign priests, about two hundred of them, nearly all Spaniards, and an order that native priests, in accord with the law, must register at government offices. He made sweeping application of the third article of the constitution, and closed the private religious schools because their teachers had no license to teach.

Now it was war between Church and State, and the bishops forbade the priests to register. The Church would not yield because it felt that the time had come to recover its privileges; the State would not yield

because it saw any retreat as restoring to the Church its political influence. On July 31, 1926, the bishops ordered the priests to cease administering the sacraments or to say mass. This amounted to a strike. The parish churches, which since the reform of 1857 had been national property loaned for Church use, were abandoned. To save them, the government promoted the establishment of committees of the faithful. In this way the churches were kept open, and the bishops found to their astonishment that the majority of Catholics—particularly the Indians for whom Catholicism was no more than an overlay on their own native rituals—did not consider the priests necessary; there were no formal services, but the churches were as full as ever. This lack of solidarity with the Roman Church persuaded Calles to abandon as unnecessary his project for the creation of a schismatic Mexican Church.

The Vatican supported the bishops, but instructed churchmen to stay out of the armed struggle, while urging on the faithful "the necessity of taking positions against parties hostile to the Church and of maintaining themselves united." In some regions, especially those around Guadalajara, Catholic guerrilla bands, which the people called *cristeros,* sprang up. The army fought them but could not prevent th guerrillas in many places from cutting out the lay teachers' tongues or killing them and setting fire to the public schools. The reprisal was fast. Six bishops were deported to Texas, and when the cristeros robbed a train, killing more than a hundred persons, there were executions of cristero prisoners. The soldiers sacked the houses of rich Catholics and even isolated the guerrilla bands, transferring peasants to other regions so that they would not be able to help the guerrillas.

Finally, the military put an end to the cristero revolution, which had spread through the states of Jalisco, Colima, and Michoacán. The bishops had never condemned it, but neither had they given their approval, perhaps because its chiefs, to attract the peasants, had adopted a somewhat radical program that included agrarian reform and nationalization of the mines. In the end, after three years, the Church submitted and the priests began to say mass again, and since that time the relations of Church and State have been normal, without any serious problems. This, after some years, made it possible for the authorities to soften the application of Article 3 and to permit the discreet reopening of Catholic schools and even of one university.

Top: General Blanco officiating at the redistribution of a vast Díaz estate. Bottom: President Calles (center) with U.S. ambassador Morrow (right).

However, from that time on, there were no more public processions, and members of religious orders and priests ceased to wear their clerical habits in public.

Calles and Obregón made a serious mistake. Fearing that no one would be able to continue their policies and also desirous of keeping power to themselves, they decided to ask congress to declare that the principle of no re-election did not mean that any person could not be elected two or more times to the presidency, but that he could not be elected twice in succession. At the same time, the presidential term was to be extended from four to six years, for it seemed to Calles and Obregón that forty-eight months was not enough time for carrying out a really substantial program. Two generals, Francisco Serrano and Arnulfo Gómez, revolted against these proposals; the revolt was crushed and they were killed. Congress approved the proposed reforms and Obregón was elected to succeed Calles. But on July 17, 1928, three weeks later, as Obregón was attending a banquet at a restaurant on the outskirts of Mexico City, a 26-year-old artist José de León Toral, approached him under the pretext of doing a portrait sketch and shot him dead. As the assassin was a fervent Catholic, the police ascribed the crime to the inspiration of Catholic groups. In addition to Toral's execution, a priest and a nun were jailed and sentenced, and the priest subsequently executed. However, many people believed that the instigators of the assassination had been leaders of the CROM, whose president, Morones, was ambitious to succeed Calles.

Calles was now in a difficult situation. In September, when the session of congress began (congress met only in the last quarter of the year in Mexico, and for the purpose of hearing the president's message and discussing the budget and proposed laws), Calles convoked all the governors, military leaders, and politicians as well and gave them a speech in which he told them that regrettable as Obregón's death was, his passing was also an opportunity for the nation. Obregón, he felt, should be regarded as the last of the caudillos, that the era of *caudillismo* had ended, and that it was time for the democratic aspiration of the revolution to be realized. He pledged not to serve beyond the expiration of his term. No one contradicted him.

That was the beginning of a period of six years during which Calles was the inspiration behind a succession of presidents. The people, in

Despite great strides toward industrialization, most Mexican workers still ply nonmechanized trades, such as the basket-weaving shown here.

a mixture of respect and jocularity, nicknamed him "el Jefe Maximo" (the Supreme Chief), although he now had no title but that of retired general and had no official post.

The choice of congress for interim president was an Obregonista, Emilio Portes Gil, ex-governor of Tamaulipas. He was to govern until the election the following year. Portes Gil did not encounter any major conflict. The CROM had lost its monopoly of the unions, and other federations were being formed around its fringes. Even relations with the United States had improved, owing especially to the friendship that developed between Calles and Dwight W. Morrow, who was appointed American ambassador in late 1927. Morrow arrived in Mexico at a time when U.S.-Mexican relations were at a low point, owing to Calles' war on the Catholic Church and his renewed attack on foreign oil interests. In December, 1925, the Mexican congress had passed a law ordering the oil companies to exchange their titles of

In an impressive show of solidarity, 200,000 Catholic protesters march along the railroad tracks from Mexico City to the basilica at Guadalupe.

ownership for fifty-year concessions; the measure was constitutional,
in accord with Article 27, but in Washington it was considered a
breach of the promise made by Obregón. American Catholic groups
and the American press magnate William Randolph Hearst, who
owned big properties in the north of Mexico, inaugurated a campaign
to defame Calles as a Bolshevik. However, the state department refused
to be influenced by them, and Morrow undertook negotiations. Within
a few weeks of his arrival, the Mexican supreme court declared the new
measure unconstitutional, thereby averting conflict. As these reversals
of policy were legalized through Mexico's own governmental machinery, Mexico's sovereignty was not damaged in the eyes of her people.

The Wall Street economic crisis of 1929 put Calles' policy of gradual
encouragement of industrialization in peril. It was necessary to increase
agricultural production to pay foreign debts, inherited from Díaz and
enlarged by the revolution. But this would be possible only if the
peasants, when the lands were given to them, also received at the same
time credits, farm implements, and livestock. For this purpose Portes
Gil's government instituted certificates of nonconfiscation, which guaranteed to the owner of an agricultural property that his holdings could
never be expropriated for incorporation into an ejido. Although many
intellectuals, some former revolutionists, and the communists regarded
this measure as a betrayal of the principles of the revolution, the truth
is that it contributed to the establishment of a measure of peace in the
rural areas and encouraged the growth of a rural middle class.

The "retired" Calles now set about to plan and organize a new
national political party to perpetuate his policies. He thought it was
not enough that the press and legislators had been granted full freedom
of speech and criticism (and did not fail to exercise it, despite the
ruthlessness of the police) but that it was necessary for the government
to be able to rely on a party that would support it. In the main, parties
had been used as tools of opposition or as a means of preparing candi-
dacies. Often they were dissolved as soon as their immediate goal had
been realized. Calles made a tour of a number of European countries,
taking note of their party machinery. Using the British Labor Party as
his model, he created, in 1929, a Partido Nacional Revolucionario (National Revolutionary Party), or PNR. "Rudimentary logic," said the
manifesto, "permits us to consider that the multiple tendencies and

opinions which presently divide the nation should be organized into two strong currents: the innovators, reformers, or revolutionaries; and the conservatives and reactionary tendency." The PNR declared its mission to be the unification of what it called "the revolutionary family."

The PNR elected its own leaders, although they generally followed Calles' guidance and regularly consulted him. The PNR was divided into three branches: workers, peasants, and the middle class. As we shall see, this party has twice changed its name, but not its basic organization; and from the time it was formed to the present, it has won all the national elections and nearly all the local ones. It is customarily called the official party and is often accused of being false to the democratic idea. But it is not the only party, since others do exist in Mexico, and neither is it a dictatorial party, because within it diverse tendencies are active. However, it is the party that always wins. Many say that its victories are the result of trickery and falsification of the results under coercion by the authorities, which is no doubt partially true. But we must take into account the fact that, at any rate, no alternative exists for those who consider themselves heirs of the revolution, for the other parties are either on the extreme right or on the extreme left.

Portes Gil's provisional government, which lasted less than a year, was characterized by intensified distribution of lands, by the lessening of the CROM's power, and by the registration of the priests (that is, the official end of the conflict with the Church); on June 29, 1929, masses were said again in all the Catholic churches of the country. As the end of Portes Gil's term approached, everything was calm.

But not for long. The PNR's favorite for candidate was a prominent industrialist, but Calles insisted on another man, an engineer who had no ties to the world of business, Pascual Ortiz Rubio. A general, Gonzalo Escobar, protested and led an armed uprising in the provinces. Calles took charge of the war department, crushed the rebellion, and at the same time ordered the execution of several communists who had taken advantage of the situation to organize soviets, following the line handed out at that time by the Communist International. It was the peasantry, supporting the army, who overcame this military revolt. Then José Vasconcelos, who had been secretary of education under Obregón, announced his candidacy on an anti-Callista platform, for he believed that the people's weariness of the unending influence of Calles would assure him victory at the polls. According to the official returns, he received 20,000 votes; he probably received many more, but still nobody believed that he had won. Vasconcelos went away to the United States, hoping that guerrilla war would break out in his favor, but nothing of the sort happened and Calles' choice, Ortiz Rubio, was proclaimed president.

Portes Gil had distributed 2.5 million acres of land. Ortiz Rubio's distribution did not exceed half a million. This was because Calles had come to the conclusion that an end should be made to agrarian reform if Mexico wanted to raise agricultural production. Many people thought Calles' growing moderation was due to the influence of Ambassador Morrow, whose house in Cuernavaca was next to Calles'. Their street, which they shared with numerous revolutionary leaders, was popularly known as the "Street of the Forty Thieves."

Ortiz Rubio was a weak man and, like many weak people, he had a sudden urge to rebel; he replaced a number of high officials who had Calles' confidence. Calles, when he found out about it, announced to the press that Ortiz Rubio had resigned, and the president, reading his political obituary in the papers, wrote his letter of resignation on the first of September, 1932. As his successor, congress named a "finger general," Abelardo Rodríguez, who was more skillful at business than at fighting. He represented a triumph for the conservative Callistas, who wanted to preserve the achievements of the revolution but to forestall further changes. Rodríguez' two years in office were characterized by an effort on the government's part to attract younger men, who had got into politics since the revolution, and intellectuals. Many of them joined the PNR and some received government posts.

In the 1934 elections, the PNR candidate was General Lázaro Cárdenas, who had played a minor role in the revolutionary fighting and was considered a loyal Callista. Two members of the opposition ran against him: General Antonio Villareal, on an anti-Callista platform, and the communist Hernán Laborde. Cárdenas made a vigorous campaign, visiting every nook and corner of the country, and formed study groups among the youthful partisans to devise a six-year plan for government. Those who voted for Cárdenas had no idea that in so doing they were closing one epoch of Mexico's history and opening another.

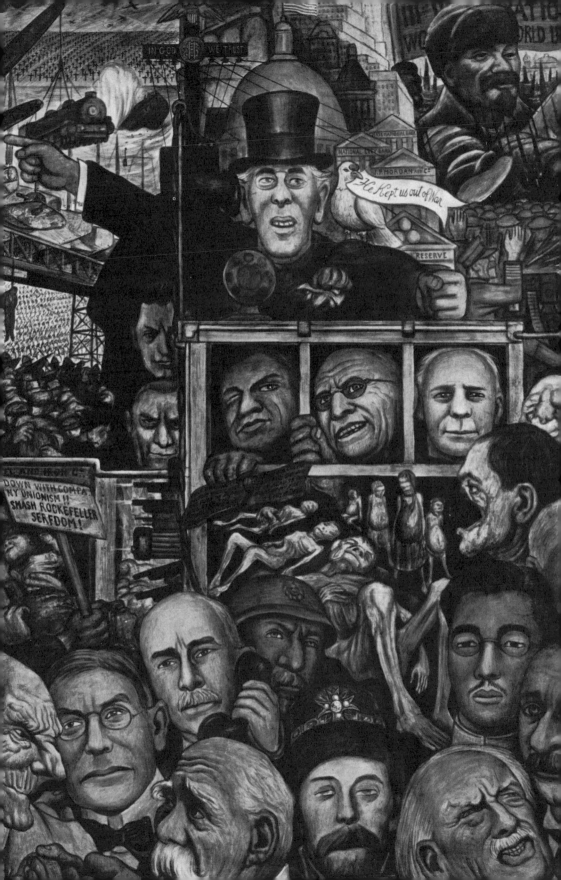

CHAPTER VIII

MEXICO'S
NEW DEAL

T he twenty-four years between the commencement of the revolution in 1910 and the election of Cárdenas in 1934 saw a new generation arise—one that had not taken part in the battles of the civil war,
and that was less pragmatic than the generation of the "finger generals," but more dogmatic and also technically better equipped. Their
numbers had also dramatically increased. From 1920 to 1935, the
population had soared from 14 million to nearly twenty, making Mexico second only to Brazil, the largest country in Latin America, in
population and wealth.

When Cárdenas took office on December 30, 1934, no one thought
that he was really going to govern, least of all Calles. The still-power-
ful Jefe Máximo had made Cárdenas president in the false belief that
he could be manipulated like the rest. Raised in a Michoacán village,
toughened by service in the armies of the revolution, a governor of his
home state, and then a cabinet minister under Calles, he had never forgotten his origins. He was not to be swayed from his conviction that
the government was morally bound to redeem its revolutionary promises, to bring the peasant something better than the exhausted farm-

*Diego Rivera's interpretation of the subverting effects of foreign economics
and political intervention are shown in this mural detail.*

land, feeble schools, nonexistent medical services, and contaminated water supply which he had known as a child. The thirty-nine-year-old reformer had close connections with the left wing of the PNR, increasingly the source of party tensions. This group of young men made up for the fact that they had not taken part in the revolution by espousing radical and Marxist ideas, but Calles flattered himself that he could pacify the group while at the same time bringing Cárdenas around to his way of thinking. Cárdenas had to take Callista candidates for the cabinet itself, but he put his own men in key places in the administration.

The new president soon proved to be more than Calles bargained for. Through his exposure to the people during the electoral campaign, he had come to realize that they were weary of Calles' shadow, and that Calles' moderate, even right-wing, position, was out of step with the electorate. A large part of the country was becoming radical because it was not receiving any of the benefits of the revolution. There were still great landholdings, the number of peons was not lessening, and the workers were restless. The professional men and intellectuals, and even the students, were disturbed about the small market for their knowledge and work. Many professional men, actually, could live only by throwing in their lot with the state, becoming bureaucrats. And they wanted a government that would create a larger, more rewarding market for their services.

Having taken account of these new tendencies (before the 1934 election), Calles had put some young men at the head of the agricultural credit banks and had made one of them, Narciso Bassols, secretary of education. Noting that, although 750,000 families had received lands amounting to 19 million acres between 1917 and 1933, there were still two million families without lands and 300 million acres undistributed, Calles appointed the PNR to draft a new agrarian code. Even though 7,000 federal rural schools had been built and illiteracy had fallen from 69 to 59 per cent, two thirds of the rural children of school age still did not go to school. Calles had seen to it that Article 3 of the constitution was amended in the direction of having the state give a socialist education, but he had not stated clearly what this was to consist of.

It was upon the discontent that Cárdenas relied to free himself from the all-powerful Calles influence. Roosevelt's New Deal had furnished inspiration to many younger men who wanted to accomplish for their country what was being done in the north. And Cárdenas was ambitious to leave his mark on the history of his country.

Promptly upon moving into the presidential palace, he began to prepare the ground for making himself independent of Calles. He speeded up the distribution of lands and personally participated in many of the title transfers to the peasants. He gave *sub rosa* orders to those who represented the government on the Board of Conciliation to favor labor as much as possible, thereby encouraging workers to strike and bring their grievances to arbitration. Calles became uneasy. He summoned to his house in Cuernavaca a number of senators who were his friends and issued a declaration which was later released to the press. He told them that there was "a marathon of radicalism" going on and that the "epidemic of strikes" was a peril for the country. Finally, he made a reference to Ortiz Rubio's downfall, as if to threaten Cárdenas with similar Callista reprisals if he did not fall into line.

Cárdenas, who had been president scarcely six months, reacted swiftly. He named Portes Gil president of the PNR, and thus put the party under his control. He shook up his cabinet, appointing men who were not considered Callistas. Little by little he eliminated the Callista governors, beginning with the governor of Tabasco, the barbarous Garrido Canabal, whose "Red Shirts" had been licensed to destroy churches, harass the faithful, and even machine-gun a group of demonstrating Catholic students. In this way Cárdenas won the Church to a neutral attitude.

The parliamentarians, realizing that Calles' power was shrinking, began to draw away from their former Jefe Maximo, who had precipitately announced that he was retiring from politics. But this was not enough for Cárdenas, whom the people had nicknamed "el Trompudo" (Snouty) on account of his prominent nose. He made use of a university professor turned union leader who had withdrawn from the CROM, Vicente Lombardo Toledano, to organize workers' demonstrations against Calles and CROM's corrupt leader, Morones. When he felt that the public was with him, Cárdenas executed a stunning *coup* in April, 1936: he ordered his agents to round up Calles, Morones, and some twenty of their gang and, under the pretext of maintaining

order, had them flown out of the country. Calles went to California, whence he returned to Mexico in 1941, and died in 1945. There was no attempt at resistance; seventeen months had been all Cárdenas needed to sap Calles' power and free himself of it.

However, Cárdenas was still under political obligation to General Saturnino Cedillo, his moderate minister of agriculture, and to Portes Gil, president of the PNR, so he replaced them. Now he began to govern his own way: saying very little indeed, keeping everyone in suspense about his decisions, traveling constantly around the country to keep in touch with the peasants, workers, and businessmen. The reporters and aides who traveled with the shirt-sleeved president returned exhausted from the presidential junkets, but Cárdenas went straight to his office to receive visitor after visitor. He did not harass anyone: neither the communists who called him "the agent of Yankee imperialism," nor the semi-Fascist army of patriot-bullies known as the "Golden Shirts," nor the newspapers that were incessantly attacking him because they feared the radicalism of his collaborators.

Illiteracy has long been a problem among the Mexican poor. Public letter writers sell their skills at sidewalk stalls.

This radicalism was purely verbal. In practice Cárdenas' policies were moderate and tended toward the same objectives as his predecessors avowed—the founding of a capitalist democratic society. The difference was that he was zealous in seeing that his government avoid the temptations that had caused earlier regimes to lose their way. Cárdenas changed the name of the PNR to PRM—Partido de la Revolución Mexicana—to prevent any other party from claiming to represent the revolution—and altered its organization, adding a fourth branch, the military. This kept the old generals quiet, giving them the illusion of sharing power. It did not prevent Cedillo, when he saw himself eliminated from government, from leading his private army in a revolt in his state of San Luis Potosí (the revolt was immediately quelled and he was killed). No other army coup has occurred since.

To create a new popular base of power, Cárdenas fostered the formation of a new union federation, the CTM (Confederación de Trabajadores de México—Confederation of Workers of Mexico), led by Vicente Lombardo Toledano, who, in his turn, in 1938 organized a Latin American union federation, the CTAL, or Confederación de Trabajadores de America Latina. A couple of years later the CTAL wound up being communist-controlled when Lombardo himself, without ever being a member of the Communist Party, became Moscow's Latin American mouthpiece.

Cárdenas tolerated this, because it gave him a leftist gloss, which he found useful against the survivals of *Callismo*. For the same reason, he modified the course of agrarian reform; as we have said, the ejido was looked upon as a transitory organization, a school for rural landowners; but Cárdenas changed it into an institution that was to be permanent, and in some cases, for instance in the cotton-raising region of Laguna, into a system for communal exploitation of the land. This was a mistake for which Mexico was to pay dearly, for it was not possible to keep on enlarging ejidos; as the population grew, the parcel each family was given to cultivate was reduced. The result was that the ejidos, which contained and still contain nearly half the arable lands of the country and employ nearly half the rural population, account for only 12 per cent of the total agricultural production.

So we see that Cárdenas—to make a better stand against Callismo—tamed the three most independent factors in Mexican politics: the congress, the unions, and the ejidos. The first was changed into a mere assembly which, ever since, has yessed the president's projects; the unions were wholly linked to the government; and the ejidos were controlled by the government through the extensive ejido bureaucracy it appointed. Playing a genuinely tutelary role to the peasants, the system delayed the apprenticeship of these rural people in landowning and in becoming farmers.

The executive branch had never been as powerful as it was under Cárdenas. For example, he was able to impose, in defiance of public feeling, a policy of systematic support of the Spanish loyalists during the civil war in Spain, not so much out of sympathy with it as because this was a chance for Mexico to affirm in the League of Nations its opposition to all intervention. The Mexican government maintained that General Franco was the product of the intervention of Germany and Italy in the civil war; for this reason and to the extent of its rather limited capabilities, it furnished arms to the Spanish Republic—nearly all acquired from the United States, which had embargoed shipment of any war matériel to Spain.

When the Spanish conflict ended, Cárdenas was able to announce, again contrary to popular feelings, that Mexico would admit a considerable number (about 25,000) of exiled Spanish Republicans, among whom were many intellectuals and technicians. These immigrants in the long run made an important contribution to the country's cultural progress and the encouragement of capitalism, despite their own leftist leanings. As they were not permitted to take jobs as manual laborers because of the de facto opposition of the unions, some devoted themselves to teaching and some to business, and they modernized both. In consequence of the new tactic approved by the Seventh Congress of the Communist International (1935), that of the Popular Front, the communists from that time on supported and praised Cárdenas. Despite this, the Mexican president invited the Bolshevik leader Leon Trotsky, who had wandered through Turkey, France, and Norway after Stalin banished him from the U.S.S.R., to spend his exile in Mexico. Trotsky, as we know, was assassinated in 1940 in his house in Coyoacán, near the capital, by a Spanish agent of the Soviet NKVD.

All these efforts to fortify the executive power, a result, let us repeat, of the desire to prevent any resurgence of Callismo, turned out to be

Workers carry the Communist Party banner during a May Day parade in 1935.

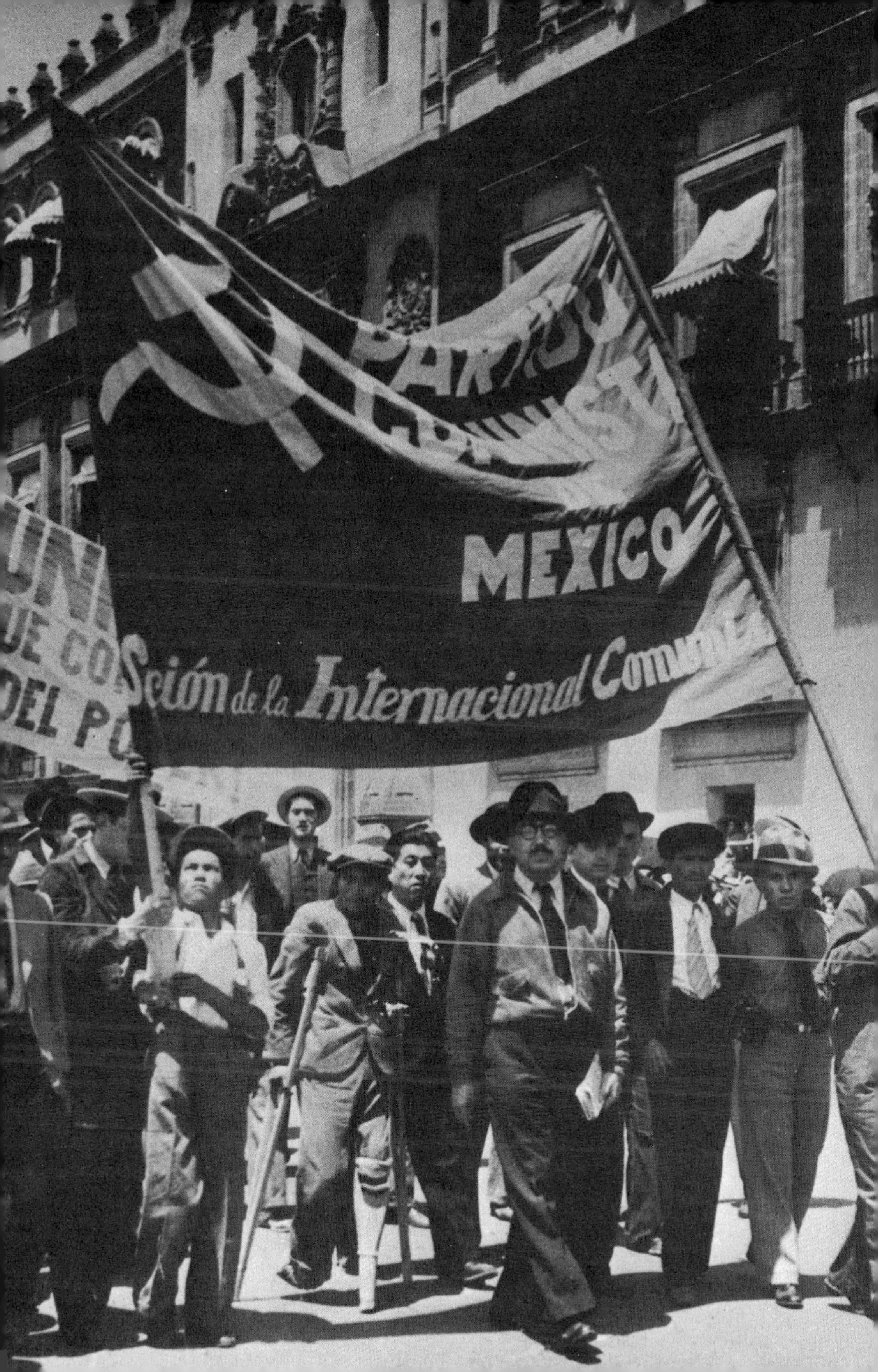
MEXICO
ción de la Internacional

very opportune politically, for in 1938, Cárdenas had to face a very serious problem. He resolved it as it would have been resolved by any other president produced by the revolution, but that did not detract from the prestige it brought him: he became a sort of hero for the left all over the world. His solution was not a matter of principle but of the necessity of preserving the national dignity as he, and the entire country, understood it. For the first time, Cárdenas found himself forming a bloc with all his people, including the conservatives and the most intransigent Catholics. The problem, as the reader may have guessed, was that of oil, and the solution Cárdenas made was nationalization of the petroleum industry. Here was the first important instance of nationalization in Latin America in modern times, and it marked out a path followed afterward by many other governments—of Latin America and other continents, leftist and rightist, constitutional and military. The history of this affair deserves to be recounted in some detail.

Though oil had been known to the Aztecs, its first commercial production in Mexico came in Porfirio Díaz' time. Oil had been discovered in the northeast, around Tampico, and that city became an oil port for the British and American companies, which between them controlled 98 per cent of the nation's output. Every attempt to organize the oil workers was firmly suppressed, and this happened even during the revolution.

The companies were now exploiting the oil lands by virtue of an agreement between Calles and Ambassador Morrow, according to which the existing concessions were recognized but further expansion was prohibited—the nation thus affirming, symbolically, its ownership of the subsoil as provided in the constitution. Whereas in 1921 one fourth of all the oil used in the world came from Mexico (neither Texas nor the Middle Eastern oil fields being extensively tapped at the time), by 1935 Mexico's production represented only one twentieth. Dissatisfied with this loss both in rank and in real production, the government established a national firm, Petroleos Mexicanos (Pemex) to discover and exploit new oil reserves.

This move had not caused any conflict between the government and the twenty-one foreign oil companies (affiliates of a few larger companies), and it was some time before the legal right of foreign companies to operate in Mexico would be reopened. Rather, the dispute

The challenging terrain of Mexican farmland, like these carefully plowed hills near Taxco, has gradually been tamed by modern technology.

when it arose had to do with labor relations. About thirteen thousand Mexicans were employed in the twenty-one oil fields, each location having its own union and its own contract with its employers. This division of the workers rendered them ineffective in gaining any improvements in working conditions or wages, and the Cárdenas government, in recognition of this failure, gave its assistance to building a more powerful central union. The National Petroleum Workers Union was formed and soon joined forces with the militant CTM, giving the scattered oil workers a leverage against their employers that they had never known.

In November, 1936, the Petroleum Union laid its demands before the companies: a single industry-wide contract with all the firms and the enforcement of the labor code of 1931 (before this, the foreign firms had arrogantly ignored the code and Cárdenas had been too preoccupied with other matters to force a showdown); wage increases; an eight-hour work day and double pay for overtime; schools for the workers and their children; paid vacations; a closed shop; and the enforced affiliation of office workers with the union. The oil firms negotiated as a unit and granted several of the demands, although they considered the wage rises that had been asked excessive and flatly refused affiliation for their clerical workers, because, they said, this would be the equivalent of opening their books to the union.

No accord was reached. The union prepared to strike, but Cárdenas decreed a waiting period of six months for negotiations. When this time had elapsed, in May, 1937, the atmosphere had become more acrimonious and the workers more impatient than ever. The union then declared that its conflict with the oil companies was not properly a strike, but an economic dispute. (The labor law provided that when there was a conflict between two parties of equal strength, a strike could be called, but that when one party was much weaker than the other, thus rendering a strike an invalid contest, the situation should be declared an economic dispute, and the conflict referred to compulsory arbitration.) Over the vigorous protests of the companies, the Board of Conciliation concurred, decreeing that since the union was very new and weak, there was no equality between the parties. The board named a committee of experts to study the situation in the oil industry so that it might arbitrate with full knowledge of the facts.

The experts—who were not without some bias—discovered that the companies were making a profit of 16 per cent as against 2 per cent then being earned in the United States. They recommended that a part of these profits gained in Mexico—half the 16 per cent—be applied to improving the living standard and working conditions of the Mexican oil workers. The experts calculated that the sum of 26 million pesos a year should go toward the cost of complying with the national labor laws and toward wage increases. The board, having reviewed the special investigators' report, decreed on August 18, 1937, that the oil firms must sign a collective contract with the union, establishing an eight-hour working day; that wage increases of 27 per cent should be granted, that clerical workers should be permitted to join the union, that a system of vacations, pensions, security, and housing should be set up, and that working clothes should be furnished to the workers.

By law any decree of the Board of Conciliation was compulsory. But the oil companies appealed to the supreme court, no doubt hoping that this would entail long delays and that the union, to speed along a settlement, would accept more moderate terms. The chief argument of the oil companies was that compliance with this decree would cost them not the 26 million pesos a year calculated by the experts, but more than 100 million, or more than their profits.

Up to that moment, the conflict had been between the firms and the workers. But when management decided not to abide by the decision of the governmental office, they converted the question into a conflict between them and the government, and put the latter in the position of either insisting upon fulfillment of the law or losing all of its moral authority. Cárdenas was certainly not the man to choose the second alternative. The heads of the oil companies, shut up in their offices in Tampico, London, and New York, did not take into account either the temperament of the Mexican president or the country's state of mind.

Formerly the public had not felt a great deal of sympathy for the oil workers, for it was feared that their gains would bring about a rise in the consumer price of oil; but the companies, in not abiding by the board's decision, had raised issues of nationalism, and popular sympathy turned toward the workers.

A kind of undeclared war ensued. The companies withdrew their accounts from the banks and Cárdenas charged them with trying to

wreck the fiscal stability of the nation. On March 1, 1938, the supreme court decided that the companies must comply with the decision of the Board of Conciliation, and the latter set March 7 as the deadline.

The companies then offered to grant the wage increases but refused to permit the office workers to join the unions. The communists and the CTM demanded that if the companies did not comply with the decree the government would take over the oil companies until they agreed to fulfill the law. No one mentioned nationalization.

Cárdenas invited the representatives of the companies to his office and told them that he considered their offer acceptable and would promise them that, as long as he was president, there would be no more demands if they complied with the law. The spokesmen for the companies asked Cárdenas to put his promise in writing. The companies had not learned their lesson from what had happened between the United States and Obregón when Washington made a similar request. Cárdenas, angry at this doubt cast on the word of the president of Mexico, rose and showed the company representatives to the door.

As soon as the public learned what had happened it was furious. The Board of Conciliation had agreed to postpone the date of compliance to the fifteenth of March. When that day arrived, the companies, still expecting Cárdenas to conciliate on a written agreement, refused to comply with the decree. According to law, they were now subject to fines equal to three months of the workers' wages.

But Cárdenas did not give in. He would not have been able to, even if he had so desired, for public anger was at white heat. Cárdenas sent a personal representative to Washington to advise President Roosevelt of the situation. But before his representative arrived, there came the companies' definite refusal to comply with the board's decree. That night, the fifteenth of March, Cárdenas called a meeting of his cabinet. In an adjoining room was a group of jurists, both of the left and the right, that he had summoned. After the meeting, he announced on the radio that, "in the national interest," he was obliged to nationalize the oil companies. Next day, the stunned companies offered to comply with the law, but it was too late. If Cárdenas had agreed, the people would have ousted him from the presidency. He did not deign to reply to the offer. For three days the jurists worked on the matter and discussed it. On the eighteenth of March the decree of nationalization was

Lázaro Cárdenas (right) and supporter Lombardo Toledano (left) are shown in a 1938 photo taken just after Cárdenas expropriated foreign oil interests.

issued. A national holiday has been observed every year since then as the anniversary of Mexican economic independence.

But enthusiasm was not a solution for everything. The situation was extremely serious. In 1935 Cárdenas had nationalized the railroads, through an agreement with the British firm that owned them, because they were bankrupt and the country was in danger of being deprived of rail communications. He turned over administration of the railroads to the unions. At the end of some months, the unions themselves asked the government to take charge of the railroads, as there had been too many emergent internal rivalries to permit efficient administration of them. After this experience, it would have been rash to hand over the petroleum industry to the unions. Cárdenas decided to turn the nationalized properties over to the state company, Pemex, already in existence but until then of minor importance.

But what was to be done with the oil itself? The ousted companies exerted pressure to prevent any foreign firms from buying Mexican oil or any foreign tankers from transporting it. To whom could it be sold? Mexico did not hesitate: Italy and Germany offered to buy it, and Cárdenas sold the nationalized oil to them, despite his avowed anti-Fascism and the fact that this oil would go, in part, to Franco's army.

The Great Powers had to be dealt with next. In Great Britain, it was easy for the Conservative Party to bring about a breaking off of relations with Mexico (they were not renewed until World War II, when London needed Mexican oil, nationalized or not). But in the United States, which had just months before declared its "Good Neighbor Policy," the companies had less luck. Although they put on a campaign that accused Cárdenas of being a communist, President Roosevelt stood by his promise. In answer to demands by American oil firms that compensation for the expropriation should be based not on their investments in Mexico but on the profits they would no longer earn on Mexican oil, Roosevelt replied, "the United States would show no sympathy to rich individual Americans who [had] obtained large land holdings in Mexico for virtually nothing . . . and [then] claimed damages for seized property." Cárdenas told his diplomats to make it clear in foreign capitals that the oil companies had obtained their concessions for minimum considerations, that they had never reinvested even a part of their profits in Mexico, that they had set up a policy of dis-

crimination against their Mexican employees, and that, finally, they
had refused to abide by the laws of the country.

The timing of Cárdenas' dramatic blow for independence was, from
the point of view of national economic stability, ill-timed, coming as it
did on the heels of the Great Depression and as Mexico was trying to
achieve so many other costly reforms. The production of oil fell still
further, and with it the income of the Mexican treasury. The oil companies also tried to prevent the buying of Mexican silver, despite the
fact that the owners of the silver mines were Americans—and in doing
so they drove the silver-mine owners to bring pressure on the White
House to accept the nationalization of oil. The oil companies were still
hopeful. They appealed to the Mexican supreme court against the law
of nationalization, but the supreme court declared it constitutional.

With that the companies came over to the idea of negotiating for
compensation. The American firms were the first to soften their line,
prodded by Roosevelt, whose government had won from Mexico the
promise (accompanied by an advance payment) to indemnify Americans who had suffered losses through the expropriation of lands. In
1940 the Sinclair Oil Company accepted the Mexican offer of 8.5
million dollars indemnity, and the front having been broken, the other
companies came into line. In November, 1941, an accord was reached
with the United States by which Mexico was to pay 40 million dollars;
but it was 1947 before a similar agreement was reached with Great
Britain, the amount being 81 million dollars plus interest. By 1956 all
the compensation had been paid.

In a movement of collective enthusiasm, immediately after the nationalization, Mexicans spontaneously joined in a grand public collec-
tion of goods to pay the debt. The rich gave money, jewelry, and other
precious objects; the poor their chickens and pigs; even the priests
handed over the golden monstrances and chalices from their churches,
an unprecedented gesture of Church support for the State. But it was
not these offerings that enabled Mexico to pay up, for well-intentioned
as the six-month-long effort was, it amounted to $440,000—about 1
per cent of the bill. Two circumstances favored the success of the
nationalization of oil and bailed the nation out of debt: first, the coming of World War II, which made Mexican oil, near at hand and sure
in supply, a precious raw material; second, the fact that the government

was able to keep Pemex out of politics. Although its director was named by the president, Pemex was not used for purposes of "patronage" or to finance political programs, but was allowed to develop as if it were a private firm. Today it furnishes an important part of the national budget, keeps oil and its by-products at a low price, which helps the industrialization of the country, and processes all its products in a series of refineries built with foreign credit of the institutional type— from the World Bank and the like. It is entirely possible that without the success of Pemex Mexico would not today be the most industrialized country of Latin America, or the one with the greatest political and economic stability.

The new national consciousness of which the expropriation of the oil companies was a product had its dramatic expression in the arts as well. A generation of intellectuals surfaced during Cárdenas' years. Called the "Contemporaries," after the title of a review in which many of its proponents were first published, the group included the poet and dramatist Xavier Villaurrutia, the dramatist Rodolfo Usigli, the poet, and later director of UNESCO, Jaime Torres Bodet, the anthropologist Alfonso Caso (who is credited with the discovery of Mixtec and Zapotec burial mounds at Monte Albán), the mural painters Rivera, Orozco, and Rufino Tamayo, and the composers Silvestre Revueltas and Carlos Chávez. One of the preoccupations of this generation is the attainment of a knowledge of precisely what constitutes a Mexican. Samuel Ramos, in his *El perfil del hombre y la cultura en México* (Profile of Man and Culture in Mexico), 1934, has tried to interpret his nation's history through an analysis of the national character. The Mexican, he said, suffers from an extreme inferiority complex stemming from centuries of colonial rule and foreign intervention. Imitation of foreign culture has produced an uncertain and unstable society which attempts to disguise its insecurities with false pride—*machismo*—both on the personal and political levels. Intellectuals have usually preferred to seek their salvation abroad—if not by emigrating, then by becoming spiritual exiles in Mexico, leaving the running of the country to their more rapacious countrymen.

Ramos' generation broke, in a measure, with that of the revolution. But it was still profoundly affected by the steady vision of the poet and Hellenist Alfonso Reyes, as it was by the flashes of anger and enthusi-

asm of José Vasconcelos. Vasconcelos, one of the few philosophers to take an active role in politics, had served under Carranza as secretary of education, initiating a vast program for education, and had later tried to run against the Callista candidate Ortiz Rubio. His autobiography *Ulises Criollo* (Creole Ulysses) made a great impression on the young. The mature were given food for thought by his *La raza cosmica* (The Cosmic Race), in which he held that the Latin American would in years to come represent a synthesis of Oriental contemplation and Occidental technology. The audience for these writings was still very limited; made up of small groups of the urban middle class, some provincial nuclei, and the students, it afforded its brightest cultural figures less acclaim than they often found in Paris or Buenos Aires.

Today Mexico is politically in the vanguard of the Latin-American countries and is showing slow but steady economic growth. Therefore, it must seem odd that such a profound and dramatic revolution as Mexico's did not have any measure of influence on Latin America, whose masses had the same aspirations and who might be expected to look to Mexico as its model. Undoubtedly it can be explained by Latin America's still-backward communications, the preponderance of strong

Despite government efforts, poverty remains a widespread affliction in Mexico. Here a group of people dwell in abandoned railroad cars.

military dictatorships, and the indifference of the Mexicans themselves to spreading their revolution to the south. Mexicans really do not feel themselves to be Latin Americans, although when they look at the map they know that they are. The process of formation of nationality is much more advanced in Mexico than in the rest of Latin America, and this makes the Mexicans feel a certain superiority to their southern neighbors, whom they consider mere imitators of Spain.

At the same time, they feel a scarcely hidden contempt for what they call *pochos,* United States citizens of Mexican origin (who they think should not have resigned themselves to becoming Americans) or dwellers in frontier regions who have adopted the life style of their northern neighbors and even their speech. In these respects, the Mexicans have retreated within themselves; and probably this "nationalism" has helped them maintain their individuality. But it is undeniable that with the presence on their border of such a powerful country as the United States, there is no small danger that Mexico, through imitation, cultural influence, intellectual osmosis, and other means, might lose her individuality and be Americanized, or "gringoized" as the Mexicans say. At any rate, the Mexican is today the most easily distinguishable national type in Latin America. There is little difference between a Peruvian popular song and one from Chile, but the difference between a Mexican popular song and one from any other Latin American country is enormous. And the same may be said of painting, music, and even language. The Spanish spoken by Mexicans contains unique elements which permit it to be identified immediately—many Hispanicized Nahuatl words and many Spanish words current at the time of the conquest but now obsolete in Spain yet still alive in Mexico. Finally, we must not overlook the tone and the melody of Mexican speech. Mexicans are quiet and have a profound musical instinct; in general they speak softly, slowly, and smoothly. Even their curses and blasphemies, of which they have an abundant and picturesque repertory, have a gentle air with more mockery than ferocity.

Cárdenas finished his term in 1940, respected on all sides and in the full blaze of glory. This did not last until his death (in 1970), because in his old age he abandoned his customary taciturnity and began to utter leftist clichés in an effort to keep himself in style with the younger men. He accepted the Stalin Peace Prize, for example, and in 1961 even offered to go to Cuba to defend Castro (an offer the Mexican government quietly prevented him from carrying out). But, for all that, the nationalization of oil entitles him to a permanent niche in the history of his country.

Perhaps because the international situation made it seem advisable, possibly because he wished his own administration as president to shine by contrast, President Cárdenas selected as the candidate to succeed him a moderate general, Manuel Ávila Camacho. Election day was marked by more than the usual violence and the results widely disputed, for the opposition candidate, the rigorous General Juan Andreu Almazán, had won great popularity among the more conservative elements and the country was convinced that he had been the winner. However, the vote count gave the victory to the official candidate.

Ávila Camacho—a moderate, a Catholic—established a breathing spell after the six years of changes and the dynamism of the Cárdenas administration. He named General Cárdenas military chief of the Pacific Coast forces (to forestall the possibility, if they were undefended, that the United States would take charge of defending them against Japan). He declared war on the Axis Powers and sent an air squadron to fight in the Pacific—a more-or-less symbolic gesture that enabled Mexico to figure among the victor countries—despite the fact that popular sympathy was with Hitler because he was a *macho* (dominant male) and because this defection infuriated the Yankees.

Ávila Camacho—perhaps because he was advised by Cárdenas— made a historic decision in 1946: he chose a civilian to be the candidate of the PRM, the official party. Thus he put an end to the era of "finger generals" and opened that of the civilian presidents. Cárdenas, without proposing to or being conscious that he was doing it, had acted as a bridge between the two epochs. He had, besides, given the oil to the country and the land to the peasants. The civilian presidents were to decide what purpose both would serve.

CHAPTER IX

THE
MEXICANIZATION
OF MEXICO

Every generation in the history of Mexico has faced huge problems. First, when the country declared its independence, the decision had to be made about what end that independence would serve, and, most particularly, how the state was to be organized—in a federal or centralist form—and what were to be the relations between State and Church. A considerable part of the nineteenth century had been dedicated to finding answers to these questions.

When the federal form of government had been established and the Church was separated from the State, other problems arose. In Porfirio Díaz' time, with industrialization, and with the formation of what political scientists nowadays refer to as the infrastructure, a decision had to be made as to who was to benefit by the nation's economic development. It was precisely because the men around Díaz decided that a small upper class—industrialists, foreign investors, and landholders —were to be the chief beneficiaries that the revolution ensued.

That event reordered Mexico's social priorities. The government that followed the revolution, headed by generals who had come out of the revolutionary struggles, gave a paternalistic and tutelary character

Two foundry workers discuss social theory in the mural "The Struggle of the Classes" by Diego Rivera, an avowed Marxist.

to this distribution of the benefits of development, and created as the instrument of this policy an official party that, without being the only one, was victorious in all the national elections and has remained in power, under various names, for half a century.

But what was Mexico to be, as a society and as a political organism? Should the country be transformed into a socialist or a capitalist state? Should democratic forms be emphasized, or, on the contrary, should the executive power be fortified and freedoms limited in order to speed up development? Should top priority be given to the encouragement of industrialization no matter what the price, or should emphasis be put on measures that would favor a certain equality among Mexicans of different classes?

These were the questions Cárdenas' successors had to answer. Obregón, Calles, and Cárdenas, and the presidents who constituted an echo of those three powerful personalities, completed the work of the revolution and consolidated it. The nationalization of oil, although pragmatic and undertaken in consequence to deal with an immediate situation, was the last revolutionary decision. From Cárdenas' regime to the present, Mexican policy has consisted in taking advantage of the conquests made by the revolution.

Five presidents, all civilians, and all holding high positions in the government, have served since 1946, the year in which the last of the "finger generals" ended his term. All acted on the premise that the revolution was, and is, irreversible. Not even the extreme right desired to return to such a situation as had prevailed before 1910. The differences between the parties, and also between those in the bosom of the official party of differing tendencies, rest precisely on the question of how to take advantage of the conquests made by the revolution and on the question of whether it is possible to go on living, politically, on revolutionary capital or—if further changes are to be carried out—in a new revolution, albeit a peaceful and nondramatic one. The polemics have been carried on not just by the politicians, but equally by the intellectuals, some youthful groups, and, partly, the technicians.

In the last few decades, Mexico's culture has made great progress, in depth as well as in breadth. The country has enough technical men and scientists for its present needs, and also has a market, though that is still limited, for its intellectual productions. There are Mexican films and Mexican theater, and some of the most important publishing firms in Latin America are Mexican. Mexico City is the Paris of Latin America. An Argentine, Peruvian, or Venezuelan artist, writer, or actor does not feel that he has triumphed until he has achieved success in Mexico City. The country has figures of universal renown: Octavio Paz, who has been the most subtle analyst of the personality of Mexico, is one of the great contemporary poets of any language; and Luis Buñuel, although he is a Spaniard in exile, has done his best work as a film producer in Mexico.

These past twenty-five years have brought a rise in Mexico's preoccupation with knowing what the Mexican really is, and there have been some harsh and bold interpretations of his personality. One widely held view sees the Mexican as divided by his Spanish origin on the paternal ancestral side and his Indian origin on the maternal. As the argument goes, the fact of being a mestizo determines his entire personality: his reactions, his sarcastic humor, his potential for cruelty, his ever-present consciousness of death, evident even in his fiestas and merrymaking; the schizophrenia of mestizo origin determines also his alternations of passivity and resignation with indignation and aggressiveness. But most Mexican intellectuals are not satisfied with this analysis. They too have tried to find, especially in very recent years, what ought to be Mexico's collective aspirations. None seems resigned to accepting the idea that the country should convert itself—as is happening—into a capitalist-democratic society. It is their opinion that development should serve for something more than reaching a greater level of prosperity—and prosperity is very far from being general. Paz has expressed this in some significant phrases:

"Some people claim that the only difference between the North American and ourselves is economic. . . . That is, they are rich and we are poor, and while their legacy is Democracy, Capitalism, and the Industrial Revolution, ours is the Counter-reformation, Monopoly and Feudalism. But however influential the systems of production may be in the shaping of a culture, I refuse to believe that as soon as we have heavy industry and are free of all economic imperialism, the differences will vanish. In fact, I look for the opposite to happen."

This preoccupation with the personality of the Mexicans and with their objectives reflects the tensions and uneasiness derived from the

Modern Mexican architects draw heavily on ancient traditions, as shown in these two buildings in the capital: (top) the library of the University of Mexico with its richly figured mosaic wall by Juan O'Gorman; (bottom) the Museum of Anthropology, in which the architect borrows the low broad profile and decorative bandings of the pyramids of earlier cultures.

profound changes taking place in Mexican society. On one hand, the old landholding class had disappeared by the end of the Cárdenas regime; there were still great landholders, true, but nearly always politicians and "finger generals," and the ownership of land did not give them any political influence. The middle class had grown enormously with the broadening of education, which created many professional men, and with the establishment of industry and commerce. The rural middle class had begun to form. This was in spite of Cárdenas' agrarian policy which retarded this development by tying to the ejidos a great part of the peasantry, who, had they received lands individually, would have swelled the ranks of this rural middle class.

The working class had grown in numbers, in specialization, and in cohesion. There were still great masses of rural and urban peons, but they were no longer virtually enslaved to the soil or to the factory. The situation of the Indian population had improved culturally as well as economically, and a large part of that population had received land. During World War II a new type of figure arose: the peon who went away to work in the United States, sometimes as a migrant farm laborer (under the worst of conditions) and sometimes in industry (under conditions somewhat better than in Mexico but below standards set for North American workers). These *braceros* (day laborers), or "wetbacks" as they were called because they entered the United States often illegally by swimming across the Río Bravo, picked up ways of life and work that once they had returned to their own country contributed to speeding up the process of modernization.

Most important, it was now possible to pass from one social group to another; the revolution had established a true social mobility, so that no one found himself ineluctably bound to a group, condemned for all his life to be a peon, a peasant, or a worker. Obviously, the great majority of peons, peasants, and workers still died belonging to the same class; but the possibility of changing one's status did exist, and the opportunities to change one's social group increased as the country became industrialized and modernized.

This modernization progressed much faster after World War II under the successive civilian presidents. In fact, Mexican politics became economic in nature, and the disputes that arose were not so much over matters of ideology as about specific economic measures.

The situation created in the Latin American market by the entry of the United States into World War II contributed to this. American industry needed raw materials, and accordingly the prices offered rose. At the same time, the United States, its industries taxed by the war effort, could no longer be the source of the many industrial products that the Latins traditionally bought, and the importation of European goods was almost entirely stopped. A result was that in some countries industries had to be quickly established to manufacture substitutes. Mexico was the first of all these countries to take major advantage of this opportunity. Chemical and pharmaceutical firms sprang up, the textile industry was diversified, the shoemaking industry was enlarged, and electrical and many other articles that had previously come from the United States and Europe were beginning to be produced at home. Even perfumery firms and French *couturier* establishments were set up in Mexico City. To the immigration of Spanish Republicans was added that of many European Jews fleeing from the Nazis. Like the Spaniards, the Jews contributed their technical knowledge, and also the special drive that exiles have when it is necessary for them to begin life all over again—and that also was a stimulus to the Mexicans.

The first wave of industrialization, however, was not very strong. It entered a noncompetitive market and could export its products also to the Caribbean islands, to Central America, and to some of the northern countries of South America. But precisely because there was no competition the quality of the products was not first-rate, the methods of production permitted were relatively costly and inefficient, and the hastily set up firms had neither adequate capital nor a large output. There was, so to speak, an inflation of new firms.

When World War II ended, Mexico, like other Latin American countries, found herself with a very impressive dollar reserve. Unlike other Latin American countries, in which these dollar reserves were used up in the importation of luxury items as soon as Europe and the United States were able to resume exporting, the Mexican government channeled a good part of them into the acquisition of capital goods. There were, it is true, many purchases of automobiles and other luxury articles, but these absorbed only a small proportion of the reserve. The great part of the balance was used to modernize or to perfect the industries hastily formed during the war.

The maker of this policy was Miguel Alemán, who had been Avila Camacho's secretary of the interior, and who was elected to the presidency in 1946. As the first civilian president and the first president of the postwar era, he formed a cabinet of "new men" of the postrevolutionary generation. His policies were directed toward the encouragement of industrialization, and for this purpose he created a number of offices that are still in existence today. The Nacional Financiera, to channel investment and to contribute public funds for the establishment of industries; the Bank of Foreign Commerce, to encourage exportation; the CEIMSA (Mexican Export and Import Company), to acquire essential products from the growers and sell them at cost, as a means of price control. He was not afraid to devalue the peso when this seemed advisable to increase exports. Many of his advisers, and Alemán himself, grew rich as a result; there is no doubt that in this period there was widespread corruption at a high level. But the graft was invested in the country itself, in the establishment of enterprises which, though they returned handsome personal profits to the investors, also created new jobs. Wine, oil, cotton, iron, and steel were produced in much greater quantities than in the past. Along the northern frontier there was very active exportation of truck-farm crops to the United States. An extensive irrigation program was begun, with a project, that of Papaloapan, very similar to the American TVA.

Here was a case of politicians who had become entrepreneurs and of entrepreneurs turned politicians, who believed in their country and at the same time in their own profits. In opposition to the traditional way, they invested in the country both their efforts and the money they took out of politics. It could be said that capitalization was accomplished by means of administrative corruption—that is, by making the public pay for it, but in a form less painful than under-consumption or higher taxes. This procedure is open to criticism from an ethical standpoint, but its efficacy had been proved in the United States in the "golden age," in the France of Louis Philippe, and in Victorian England. Mexico found herself in a stage of development similar to the boom periods of those countries, and, almost without realizing it, had recourse to the same procedures, adapted to the realities of the twentieth century.

Another reality with which Mexico had to deal was the presence, so close and so overpowering, of the United States. For Mexicans, the

saying of a writer of the preceding century remained true: "God created Mexico and the Devil created the United States." It was a devil with whom, since the time of Franklin D. Roosevelt, Mexico had established good relations. Roosevelt's visit to Mexico in 1943 was the first made by any American president while in office. On that occasion he said, "We know that the epoch of the exploitation of the resources and people of one country for the benefit of one group in another had definitely passed." The policy based on this statement made it possible for Mexico to double her gross national product during World War II, to increase by 11 per cent her economically active population, and to raise the minimum wage by 15 per cent. But this was not enough for industrialization of the country. What was needed were capital goods, machinery, patents, and the broadening of the infrastructure. Private investment went only into those activities that were most immediately profitable. For this reason the government, putting to one side the rhetoric of free enterprise, made enormous additions to its investments and thus laid the groundwork of what has come to be a form of capitalism which, if at the time it seemed to be typically Mexican, is today more and more the system of Latin America in general. Economists call it a "mixed" economy, one of public and private investment.

But this was still not enough. Foreign investment was necessary. It was Mexico's good fortune that this necessity arose at the time that a series of international institutions were being created for the purpose of aiding underdeveloped countries; institutions like the World Bank and, later, the Inter-American Development Bank. This made it possible for the nation to seek credit from these institutions and to maintain some balance with the private foreign capital that was operating in the country, for Alemán opened the doors to foreign investors—particularly those from the United States. At the same time, precisely because his sources of capital were not limited to them, he was able to establish certain rules that foreigners must observe: that no enterprise should have a foreign majority of capital, that Mexican and foreign workers should be treated with absolute equality, and, later, that an increasing number of materials of production should be made in the country. This gradual substitution of Mexican goods for imported goods was aimed at making Mexico more self-sufficient.

If this policy was to succeed, the market had to be enlarged. That

The flea market in Mexico City offers a diversity of colorful merchandise such as the religious articles and "Pre-Columbian" figures displayed here.

meant giving higher pay to the workers and speeding up formation of a rural middle class that would be able to buy industrial goods. The first requirement was met, but not the second, for the shadow of Cárdenas, determined to see his experiment with the permanent ejidos continued, prevented the government from altering its agrarian policy. However, Alemán created almost no new ejidos, and although he did distribute a great deal of land and opened up credits for the cultivation of land that had been idle, he did not turn these lands over to ejidos but to holders of small and medium-sized properties. It may be said that with this he inaugurated, discreetly, a reform of the agrarian reform. Thus he returned to the pre-Cárdenas objective of creating a rural middle class that would be capable of buying manufactured goods.

At the end of his term Alemán made the mistake of allowing friends to suggest that the constitution be modified to authorize his re-election. Although a Mexican president has enormous power and can do many things, there is one thing that is absolutely forbidden to him, not only by law but by public opinion, and that is to attempt re-election. Alemán paid for this error by having to accept as a candidate to succeed him his secretary of the interior, Adolfo Ruiz Cortines, an austere ex-book-keeper who had not been one of his inner circle.

A number of forces participated in the selection of a candidate for the presidency: ex-presidents (especially Cárdenas, who continued to have many adherents), the business group, the unions, and the peasant organizations. Alemán would have liked a successor who would carry on his policy of accelerated industrialization. But the earlier imprudence of his friends, with their unsuccessful campaign for his re-election, cost him authority and public sympathy. In the last year of his regime there was much discontent among the students, although he had built for them the splendid University City, whose campus in the suburbs of Mexico City covers some three square miles and cost more than 25 million dollars; and there was a good deal of witty comment about official corruption.

Ruiz Cortines, when he entered the Palacio Nacional in 1952, took charge of a country that was in the full course of development and whose government's funds were very low. He initiated a policy of austerity and, to a certain degree, of maintaining the status quo. The people called him "the student," since when a problem was put before him, instead of offering an immediate solution, he announced that he would have it studied. It became customary for high dignitaries to have, instead of the Cadillacs of an earlier time, old second-hand cars. Many of Alemán's projects came to a halt, the plans for irrigation were changed, and plans for great regional dams turned into plans for little canals and local dams.

With the transfer of power from the dynamic Alemán to the stand-patter Cortines, a pattern was inaugurated that seems to have taken shape since then—by which the official party, in choosing a candidate, seeks a man who is in a measure the opposite number of the outgoing president. Cortines, as we shall see, gave way to yet another dynamic personality. The official party, under Alemán, had changed its name and now called itself the PRI (the Institutional Revolutionary Party) and had also changed its internal organization by suppressing its military wing.

An austerity policy demands sacrifices, especially from the workers. This was the public sector, in which Ruiz Cortines encountered major problems. Alemán had succeeded, through friends in the labor movement, in sharply reducing communist influence in the unions; Lombardo Toledano was expelled from the CTM that he had founded. But the ideological corruption of the communists was succeeded by the bureaucratic corruption of those who took their place. This caused discontent among the workers and that, in turn, permitted the communists to present themselves as enemies of corruption and to win over some important unions, like those of the oil workers, teachers, and railroad men. They did not use this influence to fight for benefits for the workers, but to produce agitation and to organize strikes and demonstrations. The government was not able to put an end to their campaign by political means, and Ruiz Cortines' successor, his secretary of labor Adolfo López Mateos, inherited a somewhat turbulent social situation when he assumed the presidency in 1958. He threw a number of communist union leaders and intellectuals in jail (among them the painter David Alfaro Siqueiros) and they remained there all during his term of office.

López Mateos, like Alemán, was relatively young and dynamic. The economy of the country re-entered a period of expansion, the middle

class grew, and many elements of it were integrated with the *haute bourgeoisie.* He continued the policy of amortizing the ejidos, that is, of not creating any new ones, but instead fostering the ownership of small and medium-sized holdings. Some industries (telephone, electricity) were nationalized, but this nationalization was not done by expropriation, but by ordinary business deals. For this reason the process was called "Mexicanization." In some instances the government acquired the majority of the stock of various firms (for example, those of the electric power industry) and organized them into a single company under government ownership but operated commercially. Or, as in the case of the telephone industry, the government persuaded groups of Mexican businessmen to acquire the foreign-owned enterprise. And those foreign-run industries which were still permitted to sell major quantities of goods in Mexico were pressured to manufacture and assemble an ever greater number of parts within the country— as was done, for instance, with automobiles. None of this frightened away foreign investors, who continued to put their money into Mexican enterprises.

In international affairs López Mateos followed the custom established by Ávila Comacho and Roosevelt. Every Mexican president now visits his North American colleague and in turn receives a visit from the latter. He invited John F. Kennedy in 1962, an event of special importance, for in it the groundwork was laid for settlement of the only frontier problem still pending between Mexico and the United States: El Chamizal. This small territory amounting to little more than 400 acres between El Paso and Ciudad Juárez had been part of the Mexican city until 1864, when the Río Bravo (Rio Grande) changed its course naturally, leaving El Chamizal on the American side. The United States had agreed to arbitration over the disputed territory in 1911, but when it found itself losing, it withdrew from the negotiations. Now the two leaders arranged agreeable purchase terms and this piece of Mexican territory was returned. Another Mexican-American issue, that of the *braceros* who legally entered the United States as seasonal workers, was joined. The Mexican economy no longer needed the money brought home by the braceros (the profit from whom had been amply replaced by the growing gains from tourism). To satisfy the demands of the American unions, which considered these nonunion-

A colorfully shawled woman surveys her wares on Market Day in Mexico City.

ized workers an obstacle to the organization of agricultural workers in the United States and to the winning of better wages and working conditions, the American government suspended the program.

In another sphere, López Mateos followed the policy of his predecessors in attempting to broaden political participation. Ruiz Cortines had obtained passage by congress of a constitutional reform giving the vote to women. (López Mateos was the first to be elected under the widened suffrage.) López Mateos pushed through another law that allowed the various political parties a fixed number of deputies in proportion to the number of votes they obtained in national elections, so that the parties that obtained a sizable number of votes, though not sufficiently concentrated to elect their district candidates, would also be represented in the chamber. It was a kind of grafting of the proportional electoral system onto the system of district majorities. As under former presidents, different opposition parties (all parties besides the PRI are in one way or another opposition groups) enjoyed full liberty of activity and freedom to propagandize. But they did not win any important elections.

Among the outstanding parties of the era—the same parties that are still the outstanding ones today—was the Partido Popular Socialista (PPS) under Lombardo Toledano, which won 3 per cent of the votes in the last election. Its position is to the left of the PRI and in international affairs it follows the Moscow party line, but in national politics differs with the communists in that it regards as valid the programs of the Mexican Revolution, whereas the communists had wanted a socialist revolution. This party seats a small number of deputies—from two to six—in every term, but no senators, for all the senators belong to the PRI. To the left of the Popular Party is the Communist Party, which has only minimal influence upon labor but somewhat more among intellectuals and students, although the 1968 events in Czechoslovakia eroded that. There are also Castroist groups, those of the new left, and the Maoists and Trotskyites, all out of touch with the masses. They are energetic in their opposition to the Communist Party, and also have a certain amount of influence among student groups and intellectuals; from time to time they have tried to organize guerrilla groups and have failed.

To the right of the PRI is the Partido de Acción Nacional, or PAN,

Mexican piety is often expressed in the dark somber motifs of death. Here masked flagellants recreate the Road to Calvary in an Easter procession.

after the PRI the largest party in Mexico, which controls 8 per cent of the vote, and is particularly strong in the outer regions of the country (the northern states and Yucatán) and has influence among some groups of traditionalist businessmen and other members of the upper middle class. It considers the revolution irreversible, but wants more freedom of enterprise and aspires to win greater influence for the Church. To the right of this party is the Sinarquist Party, formed in Cárdenas' time as an openly Fascist group (influenced by the Spanish Falangists) but today a traditional Catholic party without any great influence save in some rural nuclei.

The PRI is composed of the labor wing (the CTM and other lesser labor federations), the peasant wing (with the CNC, or National Peasant Confederation, which is made up of the people of the ejidos and is controlled by the government through the PRI), and the popular wing (made up of different middle-class organizations). Within the PRI there are diverse tendencies—ranging from those of the survivors of the revolution, moderates today, to those of the young men, who sympathize with the new left. The PRI's apparatus functions efficiently all over the country and it has, of course, the support of the government. The Mexican president is the de facto head of the PRI and the one who names its leaders, although officially they are elected by party assemblies.

The public often grumbles at the PRI and a lot is written about the need for it to disappear or to renew itself. There have been some attempts toward rejuvenation and the formation of new programs within the PRI. But the governmental and political machine is very cautious and takes very slowly any steps toward broadening political participation. The tutelary tendency, exercised through the PRI, is still strong.

However, American students of the problem as well as Mexicans have expressed doubt that the PRI is sufficiently flexible to be the Establishment (to use the current expression) needed by Mexico in its present stage of development. They argue that the nation already has enough political maturity, and problems sufficiently complex, to need experts rather than a political machine at the helm. Their programs should evolve not from the dictates of the "revolutionary family" (which is now really the sons and grandsons of the revolutionaries) but from the will of the electorate. Nevertheless, for the present the

PRI remains the decisive political factor and has not undergone any substantial changes.

Whether the PRI was to survive, disappear, or change was the outstanding problem during the term of López Mateos' successor. Gustavo Díaz Ordaz, who was elected in 1964, proved to be a more cautious president. His term was notable for an event unusual in Mexican postrevolutionary politics. Previously the president had been untouchable; his ministers and even his policy were criticized, but never his personality. It was as if the Mexicans, intuitively realizing that their nation was still solidifying, had felt the need of symbols in which they could put their trust—the flag, for instance, and the president.

But in 1968, more than halfway through Díaz Ordaz' term, which had been characterized by the widening of the economic gap between the rich and the poor, there was an outbreak of fury, and during it the president was attacked, cursed, and booed. The Mexicans could hardly believe what occurred themselves. The flare-up happened in the course of an unimportant student conflict. But it is worth relating, for it split the country's political edifice.

The Mexican student movement had for decades been greatly divided and corrupt. It was a common thing for a professor who had ambitions to the presidency of the university to organize and finance a clique of student supporters. Strikes, fights between rival schools, and even the looting of stores were frequent during student demonstrations, and no one paid very much attention to them.

In the spring of 1968 there was such a fight between the students of two schools. The police intervened with unusual brutality, and this united the students of the two schools, along with many other sympathizers. They demanded that the chief of police be discharged. It is obvious that there must have been hidden tensions and dissatisfactions among the people, for this student protest, instead of being confined to the university, found an echo among the public, particularly after new police brutalities occurred. The previous corrupt leaders of the different student groups were discharged and a new leadership, uncorrupted and idealistic, arose from among the students themselves. The affair changed into a sort of political movement, in which everyone saw what he wanted to see: protest against the PRI, general protest against policy, dissatisfaction with the educational inefficiency of the

university system, protest at the scandalous enrichment of a certain few, against slums, and against the existence of peasants who owned no land. All kinds of grievances, until then dormant in the public mind, boiled to the surface in the heat of the student demonstrations. The students sent small groups to visit the workers' quarters and the slums. In the demonstrations in which the president was cursed there were fifty, a hundred, perhaps two hundred thousand persons. The government felt that things were getting out of hand, and was further alarmed when it considered the course of the recent French student riots. More serious violence erupted in October, 1968, on the eve of the summer Olympic Games, which were being held for the first time in Mexico. The army, which had been called in to reinforce the police, used gunfire to disperse a student demonstration in the capital's Plaza de Tlatelolco. There was talk of two hundred dead, of many people who had disappeared. Hundreds were arrested. The people were at once terrified and indignant. The impending Olympic Games afforded the government an opportunity for an appeal to patriotism ("let us not reveal our differences to foreigners") and tempers cooled, but Mexico's political life has not since returned to what it had been. Above all, the president had been taken down from his pedestal. In the second place, the army, which for a quarter of a century had not intervened in domestic affairs, had been called in to support the police; this fact might have consequences in the future, and no one felt certain that on the night of Tlatelolco the seeds of political ambition had not germinated in many a military mind.

All this, rather than being a matter of policy, had been a mistake, but one the government was obliged to defend stubbornly, for in Mexico a politician who admits a mistake is a politician done for. In other matters Díaz Ordaz followed the policies of his predecessors: in agrarian matters, he continued with the amortization of the ejidos; in industrial affairs, he proceeded with the encouragement of foreign and domestic investment. In international policy, too, he took the prescribed course.

Ever since the revolution, Mexico had tried to preserve an independent stand internationally—which, to a Mexican, meant not automatically following the lead of United States diplomacy. Hence, the Mexican government consistently refused to recognize the Franco gov-

Government reforms did not satisfy these farm workers who are staging a demonstration in Mérida, the capital of Yucatán.

ernment in Spain, for it regarded the existence of that regime as the result of foreign intervention, and for the same reason refused to break off relations with Cuba when the Organization of American States decided to do so. Mexico was, until 1971, the only Latin American country in which Cuban planes touched down and from which one could go freely and directly to Cuba. This attitude did not derive from sympathy for the Castro regime, which the Mexican government had never felt, but from the desire to preserve the independence of Mexican diplomacy which had many times shown its commitment to the policy of nonintervention. Washington understood this and made no attempt to bring official pressure on Mexico or change her attitude, pressure that would only have resulted in entrenching the government in its independent position or, had Mexico bent to the United States, in provoking general contempt in the country. This independent posture was one Mexico had also shown in relation to the government in Guatemala in 1954, when the regime of Jacobo Arbenz-Gúzman was

A scene in Mérida, where old horse-drawn wagons still serve the taxi trade

accused of being pro-communist and Mexico refused to condemn it. Another gesture of independence was inviting General de Gaulle to visit Mexican soil when he was president of France. Mexico has never broken off relations with the U.S.S.R. (save for a short period under Calles), although it has not hesitated to expel Soviet diplomats when it considered that they were interfering in internal affairs.

Today, the things that trouble Mexicans and their government more than international or strictly economic questions are precisely those domestic problems that center upon the possible evolution of the political system. It does not seem possible to continue with the old system by which the government gives subsidies (discreetly but not secretly) to the opposition to support its newspaper and electoral campaigns, and neither does it seem possible that anyone who wishes really to make waves in politics should still have to do so through the PRI if he expects to produce any real effect. But, at the moment, nobody seems able to offer an alternate system, and the existing parties have no real attraction for the public, which regards them all as subject to or appendages of the PRI. But recently there have been some surprises in local elections in which the PAN has won, probably not so much because of its rightist position as because of its opposition to the PRI.

The Mexican political regime has been compared to that of Turkey. But, say defenders of the PRI, in Turkey, when an opposition party won, the election result was chaos, which gave the army a pretext for entering politics and seizing power. This, they add, can be avoided in Mexico only by means of the PRI. Those who demand more democracy have a handicap: they express sympathy for regimes outside Mexico that are indubitably less democratic than Mexico's—like those of Cuba, China, and the Soviet Union—so that the PRI continues to be the only alternative. And possibly this, which is good for the country on a short-term basis, may not be good for it on a long-term one.

In any case, in June, 1970, the PRI brought about the election of its candidate, Luís Echeverría, who was Díaz Ordaz' secretary of the interior. His government is made up of young technical men, who are little known. They are trying to be a rejuvenating element in the country's economic life, but no one knows how far they will be able to go in trying to solve the problems they face. Basically, they attempt to convince the privileged classes to accept some better distribution of the wealth in order to prevent any social explosions in the future.

Mexico is no longer in a position to be considered an underdeveloped country; she is on the way to full development although there are large underdeveloped areas in her territories (in the south and in a section of the center) and much backwardness among her population (chiefly, the illiteracy and lack of technical skills among peasants and urban slum dwellers). Mexico stands today as the Latin American country with the greatest degree of industrialization, with the greatest social mobility, and the greatest political stability. Among the countries of the world she is one that has had a very high and very steady annual rate of economic growth—from 5 to 7 per cent, for nearly two decades. Mexico has almost no uncontrolled inflation (there is some partly controlled inflation). Her economy has become diversified and she buys and sells with more countries than she did twenty years ago, when she depended almost exclusively on the United States; but on the whole her principal supplier and biggest customer is still her northern neighbor. Already Mexico has moved out of the classification of exporter of only raw materials; one fifth of her exports are now manufactured goods. Her bond issues for the financing of nationalized enterprises are quickly taken up by the financial markets of western Europe and the United States, and her unit of currency, the peso, is sufficiently stable for the International Monetary Fund to include it among the supporting currencies.

The gross national product has increased twenty-four times between the years 1921 and 1968. Industrial production has increased three times faster than agricultural production, which is still poorly managed and lacking technical assistance. Building construction has increased thirty-five times and electrical output fifty times.

Alongside the positive features are other negative ones. First of all, there is the persistent problem of great segments of the population who live at the poverty level, a level much lower in Mexico than in the United States, and as a corollary the increase in inequality of income among the different social classes. Furthermore, the foreign debt is considerable, and a fourth of the annual income in foreign currency has to be used to pay off the principal and interest on loans that were floated earlier—a total of 4.5 billion dollars. But the long-standing problem, which conditions all the others, is the growth of population,

The proud and lonely figure of a village priest on his appointed rounds near Veracruz suggests the dignity and determination of the Mexican people.

at a rate of 3.5 per cent a year, and its unequal distribution. (From 1940 to 1960 the rate of population increase was 2 per cent.) If we take into account the fact that every new job requires a capital investment of about $8,000, we shall understand the magnitude of the problem. This is aggravated by the fact that birth control campaigns cannot count on governmental support (although they are not prohibited) and seem to evoke little interest among the poorest sectors, which are those with the highest birthrate. Solution is not made any easier by the fact that as the industrial sector develops and modernizes, it requires a proportionately smaller work force. This fact gives one more argument favoring the urgency of greater agricultural development, which uses a larger percentage of labor. Of course, Mexico has desperate need of higher farm productivity, just to feed its people—a third of the population suffers from malnutrition!

Of the 48 million Mexicans alive today, more than seven million dwell in the capital, which makes the country a kind of macrocephalic monster. Only one of the provincial cities, Guadalajara, has reached a million in population. At the present rate of population growth, the country will double every twenty years. In the year 2000, therefore, Mexico will have about 100 million inhabitants.

All this causes imbalance in the industrialization and in the development of the different regions of the country. Life in Mexico City, for that matter, is as difficult and uncomfortable as in any big city of any other country. The flood of population growth not only emphasizes the social inequalities (enough schools, hospitals, and so forth have never been built)—which government action tries to palliate by social security, pensions, the subsidized sale of essential goods at low prices, et cetera—but also augments class differences. Thus Mexican society today is composed of an upper class of great landholders and great industrialists—which constitutes 5 per cent of the population—and a well-to-do middle class of landholders, industrialists, merchants, professionals, and technicians—which makes up 11 per cent. Farther down there is the middle class proper—bureaucrats, teachers, small farmers, and merchants—which takes up 19 per cent. There remains 65 per cent, which includes the workers and, below them, the peasants and slum dwellers.

Mexico is in a relatively favorable condition for facing her problems.

She now enjoys political stability and does not at the moment appear threatened by militarism. There is a growing brain pool, collaboration with the United States is satisfactory, and just at present the political system is working smoothly, although perhaps not as well as a few years ago. But any decline in advancement, any grain of sand that alters the functioning of the governmental and economic machinery, could bring to the surface the social tensions submerged in Mexican society. However, the national personality of the country has never been so well developed as at present, and this, doubtless, will aid in the finding of original solutions, Mexican style, to these problems.

How has it come about that Mexico finds herself in such a privileged situation, despite all the problems she faces, as compared to the other Latin American countries? To say that it is owing to political stability, the mixed economy, or to industrialization would be simply to pose the question of why Mexico has been able to industrialize herself more rapidly, or obtain more political stability, or create a mixed economy. I think the final answer must be sought in the fact that Mexico is the only Latin American country that, up to the present, has succeeded in destroying the chief obstacles to the solution of her problems. The future will show whether the new problems of today, which are the outcome of just that prosperity and stability, can be overcome without shakeups or whether they lead to further turmoil. What is certain is that Mexico, strong in her historical experience, will not be content to leave her problems unsolved.

CHRONOLOGY

3000–1500 **B.C.**	Nomadic tribes begin cultivating corn (maize)
300–200	Olmecs settle at Monte Albán in the Oaxaca Valley
A.D. c. 300–c. 900	Mayan culture flourishes; temples and cities are built
c. 800–c. 1100	Toltecs invade the central plateau; later dominate Yucatán
1200–1521	The Aztec civilization and empire
1325	The Aztecs found Tenochtitlán (Mexico City)
1428–1440	Reign of Itzcoatl; formation of the Aztec League
1441	Rebellion of the Mayas against the Chichimecs
1502–1520	Reign of Montezuma II
1517	Hernández de Córdoba discovers Yucatán
1519	Hernán Cortés arrives in Mexico and founds Veracruz
1520	Aztecs drive the Spaniards from Tenochtitlán
1521	Spaniards conquer Tenochtitlán and end the Aztec Empire
1521–1821	Mexico is a Spanish colony
c. 1522–c. 1550	Conquistadors subjugate the natives of Mexico; cities are founded; development of the mining industry
1535	Mexico is organized as the viceroyalty of New Spain
1553	The University of Mexico opens
1557	Bartolomé de Medina invents a new silver mining process
1598	Mexico's first effective Indian insurrection occurs among the Tepic miners
1720–1722	Spaniards occupy Texas
1808–1813	Creoles fight for the sovereignty of New Spain
1810–1811	Miguel Hidalgo leads the first major rebellion against Spanish rule; it fails and Hidalgo is executed
1813–1815	José María Morelos leads the revolutionary forces; calls the first Mexican congress, which declares independence; and serves as president until he is executed
1816–1821	Spanish rule is re-established, guerrilla warfare continues under Vicente Guerrero
1821–1823	Agustín de Iturbide leads conservative groups in seeking independence; his Iguala Plan calls for a constitutional monarchy, and he names himself emperor
1824	Mexico becomes a federal republic with Guadalupe Victoria as its first president
1833–1855	Antonio López de Santa Anna dominates Mexican politics; a highly centralized government is established
1835–1836	American colonizers of Texas proclaim a republic; Santa Anna wins the Alamo but is captured at San Jacinto
1838	A French expedition occupies Veracruz in the "Pastry War"
1845	The United States annexes Texas

1846–1848	War between the U.S. and Mexico ends with the Treaty of Guadalupe Hidalgo in which Mexico cedes disputed lands
1853	The U.S. buys the Mesilla Valley in the Gadsden Purchase
1857–1860	Civil war in which liberals triumph over conservatives; Benito Juárez becomes president
1861–1862	France, Spain, and Britain occupy Veracruz upon Mexico's inability to pay foreign debts
1864	Archduke Maximilian installed as emperor of Mexico
1867	Maximilian is executed; Juárez is re-elected president
1873	A railroad opens between Veracruz and Mexico City
1876–1911	Porfirio Díaz is virtual dictator of Mexico; order is established, finances stabilized, industries developed, repression of Indians and the working classes
1890–1910	Period of social unrest, agrarian uprisings, and strikes
1910	Francisco Madero organizes a revolt; the era of the Mexican Revolution begins
1911	Díaz is overthrown; Madero is elected president
1913	Victoriano Huerta seizes power
1914	Venustiano Carranza ousts Huerta and becomes president
1915–1916	Civil War in which Carranza and Álvaro Obregón triumph over Emiliano Zapata and Francisco (Pancho) Villa
1917	Congress promulgates a new reformist constitution
1920	Obregón ousts Carranza and is elected president
1924–1933	Plutarco Elías Calles dominates Mexican affairs
1926–1929	Insurrection of the Catholic Church against the Revolution and the government
1929	Formation of the National Revolutionary Party (PNR)
1931	Mexico joins the League of Nations
1934–1940	Presidency of Lázaro Cárdenas; adoption of a Six-Year Plan of social legislation and economic development
1937	Nationalization of the railroads
1938	The government expropriates American and British oil companies; the PNR is transformed into the Party of the Mexican Revolution (PRM)
1940–1946	Presidency of Manuel Ávila Camacho
1942	War is declared on the Axis Powers
1943	Social Security is established; Roosevelt visits Mexico
1946–1952	Presidency of Miguel Alemán Valdés; economic expansion and widespread corruption
1952–1958	Presidency of Adolfo Ruíz Cortines
1953	Woman suffrage is granted
1958–1964	Presidency of Adolfo López Mateos
1964–1970	Presidency of Gustavo Díaz Ordaz; student riots
1968	The Olympic Games are held in Mexico City
1970	Luís Echeverría becomes president

CREDITS AND INDEX

Page numbers in **boldface type** refer to illustrations.
Page references to map entries are in *italic type.*